EAT
YOURSELF
TO ENERGY

EAT YOURSELF
TO ENERGY

INGREDIENTS & RECIPES
TO POWER YOU THROUGH THE DAY

GILL PAUL

NUTRITIONIST: KAREN SULLIVAN, ASET, VTCT, BSC

hamlyn

An Hachette UK Company
www.hachette.co.uk

First published in Great Britain in 2014 by Hamlyn,
a division of Octopus Publishing Group Ltd
Endeavour House
189 Shaftesbury Avenue
London WC2H 8JY
www.octopusbooks.co.uk

Distributed in U.S. by Hachette Book Group USA,
237 Park Avenue, New York NY 10017 USA
www.octopusbooksusa.com

Distributed in Canada by Canadian Manda Group,
165 Dufferin Street, Toronto, Ontario,
Canada M6K 3HG

ISBN 978-0-600-62704-3

A CIP catalog record for this book is available from
the Library of Congress

Printed and bound in China

10 9 8 7 6 5 4 3 2 1

All reasonable care has been taken in the
preparation of this book but the information
it contains is not intended to take the place of
treatment by a qualified medical practitioner.

People with known nut allergies should avoid
recipes containing nuts or nut derivatives,
and vulnerable people should avoid dishes
containing raw or lightly cooked eggs.

Standard level kitchen spoon and cup
measurements are used in all recipes.
Ovens should be preheated to the specified
temperature—if using a convection oven,
follow the manufacturer's instructions for
adjusting the time and temperature. Medium eggs
should be used unless otherwise stated.

Some of the recipes in this book have previously
appeared in other titles published by Hamlyn.

Editor: Jo Wilson
Copy-editing: Jo Smith
Art Director: Jonathan Christie
**Photographic Art Direction, Prop Styling
and Design:** Isabel de Cordova
Photography: Will Heap
Food Styling: Joy Skipper
Picture Library Manager: Jen Veall
Assistant Production Manager: Caroline Alberti

CONTENTS

INTRODUCTION

Do you drag yourself out of bed in the morning, yawn all through the working day, and find it hard to concentrate, then collapse in front of the television in the evening, unable to face making a meal, let alone doing the dish washing afterward? Would you like to become one of those people who jogs in the park, goes to the theater, and regularly cooks dinner for friends, but you just don't have the stamina on top of your other commitments?

Lack of energy is a common complaint in the twenty-first century, partly because modern technology means we are constantly on call to deal with work and family crises in a way that previous generations weren't. But there are also a number of physical reasons why you might be feeling rundown and lethargic (see box opposite, Why you may lack energy).

When we are feeling exhausted, many of us are tempted by energy bars and sports drinks. The trouble with these instant fixers is that they are full of sugar and will give you only a temporary boost. This boost will be followed by a huge drop in energy levels when your pancreas releases insulin to deal with the excess sugar in your blood. Like coffee, another crutch when you are feeling weary, sports drinks also tend to contain caffeine, which increases the release of the stress hormone adrenaline—fine when you need to run the 100 yards but not so good when you're stuck in a tedious meeting or picking kids up from school.

This book shows you how to eat yourself to energy by choosing foods that keep blood sugar levels steady and address the causes of low energy. The recipes contain all the vitamins, minerals, and trace elements you need to ease niggling health problems and make you feel in tip-top shape and raring to go.

Why you may lack energy

- If you have been worried about low energy for a while, ask your doctor to run blood tests to rule out conditions, such as anemia or an underactive thyroid gland, both of which will undermine your energy levels.
- It's easy to be low in essential vitamins and minerals if you eat a diet that contains a lot of processed foods, which have been stripped of their key nutrients. Even slight deficiencies can affect your energy levels.
- If you lead a stressful lifestyle and tend to run on adrenaline, your adrenal glands can become exhausted, while vital organs are not getting the nutrition they need because your body is constantly in emergency mode. Women tend to feel more tired than usual in the runup to their periods and during the menopause. It is important to eat the right foods to balance hormone levels.
- A candida yeast infection in the digestive system may cause your energy levels to drop. This is often caused by the repeated use of antibiotics. Ask you doctor to run tests if you think you may have a candida infection.
- Other factors that affect energy levels include depression, weight-loss diets or being overweight, chronic pain, ME (chronic fatigue syndrome), and digestive disorders, such as constipation.

How to eat yourself to energy

1. Eat a lot of good-quality protein

Protein is required for the production of energy and keeps you going for longer than carbohydrate foods. It is beneficial to eat protein before exercise, and it doesn't cause the blood sugar highs and lows that you can get from refined carbohydrates found in sweet foods and white flour products. That's why it's far better to have a boiled egg as a midmorning snack than a doughnut or Danish pastry.

2. Eat plenty of fish

Fish is a low-fat, concentrated source of protein, full of omega-3 oils that are essential for energy production and also help to balance blood sugar levels. All types of fish are immensely nutritious.

3. Choose the right carbs

Choose carbohydrates that are low in the glycemic index, a list that rates foods according to their effect on blood sugar levels. High-GI carbohydrates (such as sugar and sweet-tasting foods, white bread, potatoes) will make blood sugar levels rise rapidly then fall again, causing energy dips. Low-GI carbohydrates

(whole grains, vegetables, and beans) give steadier energy levels.

Choose whole-wheat bread, rice, pasta, and cereals, as well as a variety of beans (which also happen to be rich in protein). These are good sources of the B vitamins, which help to support the nervous system in times of stress, as well as fiber to keep the digestive system functioning smoothly and your blood sugar levels stable.

4. Support your liver

It's important to support the liver so it can perform its multiple roles of removing toxins from the blood, balancing hormone levels, and assisting the digestion of food. Choose plenty of leafy green vegetables, berries, onions, and yogurt with live active cultures. Tobacco, caffeine, and alcohol challenge the liver and deplete energy, so when you are struggling with fatigue it's best to avoid them altogether.

5. Get enough iron

Iron (found in oysters, beef, turkey, dried fruit, and leafy green vegetables) should be eaten in combination with vitamin C to improve uptake by the body. It boosts the levels of hemoglobin cells in the blood, which carry the oxygen to muscles and organs, allowing them to convert nutrients into energy.

6. Include iodine in your diet

The thyroid gland needs ample iodine for normal function, and even a slight deficiency can slow you down. That's why you should eat plenty of foods containing iodine (such as seaweed, eggs, shellfish, and yogurt with live cultures). Avoid overdoing soy products and don't eat excessive quantities of brassica vegetables (cabbage, broccoli, cauliflower, and kale) if you are even slightly deficient, because they can block iodine uptake.

7. Take steps to prevent candida

Some experts think candida yeast infections in the digestive system can lead to low energy and recurrent headaches. To prevent one taking hold, it's worth following a few ground rules. Cut right back on sugar, avoid alcohol, and ease off foods that ferment in the upper digestive tract, such as mushrooms, refined carbohydrates, and vinegar. Eat plenty of plain yogurt with live cultures to replenish the healthy bacteria in your digestive system.

8. Improve your sleep

Choose foods that will improve the quality of your sleep. Tryptophan is a key amino acid that aids restful sleep (good sources include turkey, chicken, tuna, tofu, and kidney beans), while magnesium (found in nuts and leafy green vegetables) helps to relax the nervous system and allow you to nod off.

9. Choose foods to lift mood

Lack of energy is a common symptom of depression, but certain foods (including turkey, salmon, and cocoa) promote the release of "happy hormones," such as serotonin, which can lift low moods.

10. Keep up the fluids

Drinking plenty of water is essential for good energy levels. Herb teas are also recommended, but avoid fruit juice on its own as it pushes up blood sugar levels.

Getting started

You'll feel better as soon as you start eating the right foods and cut back on foods that make you sluggish. Follow the two-week plan on pages 30–33 for a comprehensive approach, or check the problem solver section (see pages 26–29) and focus on foods recommended for the particular causes of your low energy. On pages 12–25, you'll find advice on how to include the most effective functional foods in your diet.

It may sound counterintuitive, but exercise actually gives you energy, so try to incorporate some into your lifestyle. Regular exercise will reduce your levels of stress hormones and promote the release of feel-good endorphins, as well as stimulate the supply of oxygenated blood to your tissues and promoting restful sleep.

There are many other benefits to be gained by following the advice in this book. If you're overweight, you will start to lose the excess weight in a gradual and sustainable fashion. If you've been dependent on caffeine, smoking, or alcohol, the foods in this diet will help to reduce your cravings for them. You'll also notice that regular aches and pains, including headaches and stiffness, are a thing of the past, and that your energy levels don't rise too quickly or slump between meals. You'll feel healthier all round— and it won't take long to rediscover your get-up-and-go attitude.

ENERGY
SUPERFOODS

SUPERFOODS

For sustained energy without any slumps, include the following powerful foods in your diet.

Cocoa

✔ Boosts energy
✔ Enhances concentration
✔ Lifts mood
✔ Balances blood sugar levels
✔ Helps kick addictions
✔ Increases supply of oxygenated blood
✔ Promotes liver health

Cocoa is one of the richest sources of antioxidants. It contains chemicals that can help to ease depression and the symptoms of stress. Buy a brand that is unsweetened, 100 percent pure cocoa powder.

It's rich in ...

→ Magnesium, encouraging energy, reducing sluggishness, and addressing mood swings
→ Iron, necessary for the production of oxygen-carrying red blood cells
→ Anandamide, which raises levels of serotonin, endorphins, and dopamine, all of which help you to relax and lift your mood
→ Flavonoids, which help to reduce insulin resistance and stabilize blood sugar levels

Use in ... chili con carne and other beef dishes to enhance flavor; use in warm chocolate sauces and drinks; add to banana smoothies with a little honey to sweeten; bake in cakes, cookies, and desserts.

SEE: COCOA & CINNAMON-COVERED ALMONDS, P. 60; FLAXSEED & COCOA BITES, P. 61; BEET BROWNIES, P. 124

Kale

✔ Balances blood sugar
✔ Boosts production of red blood cells
✔ Raises energy levels
✔ Supports liver function
✔ Promotes health of the adrenal glands
✔ Regulates hormones
✔ Helps overcome addictions
✔ Boosts immunity

Kale is one of the best plant sources of calcium, which encourages a healthy sleep cycle and supports the activity of the nervous system. One study found that eating a diet rich in vitamin E, of which kale is a great source, reduces the risk of developing diabetes by about 30 percent. Avoid eating in large quantities if you have an underactive thyroid gland (see page 27).

It's rich in ...
→ Calcium, encouraging restful sleep and aiding nerve function
→ The B vitamins, easing fatigue, anxiety, and depression, and boosting concentration and energy levels
→ Iron, encouraging the production of oxygen-carrying red blood cells
→ Vitamin C, boosting immunity, helping prevent damage to cells as a result of stress, and encouraging a healthy metabolism

Use in ... soups, stews, and casseroles; steam and top with grated lemon zest, sea salt, and olive oil; add to whole-grain pasta with a light pesto and a good grating of Parmesan cheese; roasted with a little sesame oil and serve as chips; stir-fry with mushrooms and cashews.

SEE: HEARTY KALE SOUP WITH GARLIC CROUTONS, P. 75; CREAMY KALE, WHITE BEAN & ROSEMARY SOUP, P. 76

Rosemary

✔ Lifts mood
✔ Enhances concentration
✔ Improves memory
✔ Offers pain relief
✔ Encourages digestion
✔ Supports liver function
✔ Provides energy for exercise
✔ Reduces sluggishness
✔ Boosts immunity

Rosemary has a long tradition of use as a stimulant; one study found that simply sniffing the herb promotes alertness and improves memory. It's rich in key minerals and antioxidants that promote overall health and, in particular, target the brain, liver, and immune system.

It's rich in ...
→ Vitamin A, for healthy immune and nervous systems
→ Carsonic acid, an antioxidant that protects brain cells and tissues and improves memory
→ Anti-inflammatory agents, such as rosemarinic acid, which reduce pain; for example, headaches and muscle pain
→ Folic acid and other B vitamins, which encourage nervous system health, promote healthy metabolism and energy levels, and balance blood sugar levels

Use in ... omelets and frittatas; use to season chicken and lamb stews; roast with new or sweet potatoes with a little olive oil and garlic; steep in olive oil and use as a dip for whole-grain breadsticks; roast with butternut squash and goat cheese.

SEE: BAKED PUMPKIN & GOAT CHEESE, P. 92; BRAISED TURKEY WITH YOGURT & POMEGRANATE, P. 109; FIG & WALNUT UPSIDE-DOWN CAKE, P. 125

Blackberries

✔ Boost immunity
✔ Encourage healthy digestion
✔ Ease constipation
✔ Balance blood sugar levels
✔ Relieve pain
✔ Promote healthy liver function
✔ Regulate hormones

....

High in immune-boosting vitamin C and rich in fiber, blackberries raise energy and lift mood while supporting overall health. One study found that the antioxidants contained in blackberries and other purple, blue, or red fruit fight inflammation related to chronic pain, including headaches and arthritis.

....

They are rich in ...
→ Anthocyanins, powerful antioxidants that improve health on all levels and ease inflammation
→ Fiber, balancing blood sugar levels and encouraging healthy digestion and liver function
→ Phytonutrients that can help to balance hormones and relieve symptoms of premenstrual syndrome (PMS) and menopause
→ Vitamin K, which is required for a healthy nervous system and brain function

....

Use in ... fruit salads; add to leafy green salads with toasted pecans and feta cheese; use in crisps and fruit compotes; blend with fresh yogurt and honey for a mood-lifting smoothie; roast with pork.

....

SEE: BLACKBERRY BREAKFAST BARS, P. 39;
BAKED APPLE & BERRY QUINOA, P. 42; FRUITY
FROZEN YOGURT, P. 112; PEAR & BLACKBERRY
CRISP, P. 117; HOT BLACKBERRY & APPLE
TRIFLE, P. 118

Avocado

✔ Supports liver function
✔ Helps reduce pain
✔ Lifts mood
✔ Encourages restful sleep
✔ Eases symptoms of stress
✔ Boosts immunity
✔ Balances blood sugar
✔ Enhances memory

....

Recent studies have found that eating avocado regularly improves liver health. The healthy fats and proteins contained in avocado can also boost your metabolism, lower cholesterol, and provide a sustained source of energy to keep you going.

....

It's rich in ...
→ Potassium, for a healthy nervous system and pain management
→ Magnesium, which reduces the release of the stress hormone cortisol, regulates nerve function, and aids restful sleep
→ Glutathione, which is necessary for the liver to cleanse harmful toxins
→ Fiber, balancing blood sugar levels and promoting healthy appetite and digestion

....

Use in ... place of butter or mayonnaise in sandwiches; use in grilled vegetable wraps with fresh tomato salsa; add to tomato and onion salads; use in guacamole, served with fresh crudités; add to smoothies with fresh berries and bananas; use in salads, topped with grilled scallops.

....

SEE: AVOCADO HUMMUS, P. 52; BROWN RICE &
QUINOA SUSHI ROLLS, P. 56; SMOKED CHICKEN
WITH BEANS, WALNUTS & TARRAGON, P. 83;
TURKEY BURGERS WITH SPICY SALSA, P. 90

Walnuts

✔ Balance hormones
✔ Regulate blood sugar levels
✔ Ease cravings
✔ Reduce muscle and overall fatigue
✔ Encourage healthy sleep patterns
✔ Boost energy

One of the best sources of phytoestrogens (natural plant estrogens), walnuts are particularly good at balancing hormones in women, leading to enhanced energy levels and an increased sense of well-being. Walnuts also contain tryptophan, boosting mood and energy, while aiding restful sleep.

They are rich in ...

→ Arginine and glutathione, which support the activity of the liver
→ Omega-3 oils, preventing surges in stress hormones and encouraging brain health
→ Magnesium, which reduces muscle fatigue, boosts immunity, and promotes relaxation
→ High-quality protein, helpful for increased energy levels

Use in ... leafy green salads with dried cranberries, apples, and goat cheese; add to sweet and savory crumb toppings; stir into chicken salads with Greek yogurt and lemon zest dressing; add to spicy rice dishes; serve with roasted beets; add to cakes and breads.

SEE: BAKED APPLE & BERRY QUINOA, P. 42; FLAXSEED & COCOA BITES P. 61; APRICOT & WALNUT OAT BARS, P. 62; SMOKED CHICKEN WITH BEANS, WALNUTS & TARRAGON, P. 83; PEAR & BLACKBERRY CRISP, P. 117; BEET BROWNIES, P. 124; FIG & WALNUT UPSIDE-DOWN CAKE, P. 125

Quinoa

✔ Lifts mood
✔ Eases anxiety
✔ Encourages restful sleep
✔ Balances blood sugar levels
✔ Reduces fatigue
✔ Balances mood swings
✔ Encourages red blood cell production
✔ Provides energy for exercise
✔ Eases chronic pain

Quinoa is an incredibly nutritious, protein-rich seed that is packed with the B vitamins, fiber, and iron to lift energy levels and mood, and keep them stable throughout the day.

It's rich in ...

→ Tryptophan, which increases the levels of serotonin to calm the nervous system
→ Melatonin, encouraging restful sleep and healthy sleep patterns
→ Lysine, helping your body absorb nerve-supportive calcium
→ Fiber, which balances blood sugar levels, supports liver function and healthy digestion, eases constipation, and stabilizes mood

Use in ... soups, casseroles, and stews to provide texture and nutty flavor; use in place of rice or couscous in salads and as a bed for curries, stews, and roasted vegetable dishes; serve with tarragon and steamed edamame (soybeans); serve warm with scallions, lime, and cilantro; bake in healthy loaves and cakes with dried fruit and nuts.

SEE: BAKED APPLE & BERRY QUINOA, P. 42; BROWN RICE & QUINOA SUSHI ROLLS, P. 56; BUTTERNUT SQUASH STEW WITH HERB QUINOA, P. 96

Halibut

✔ Stabilizes blood sugar
✔ Reduces hunger and cravings
✔ Eases symptoms of stress
✔ Eases anxiety and depression
✔ Fights fatigue
✔ Encourages heart health
✔ Raises energy levels
✔ Supports the liver
✔ Boosts cognitive function

Halibut is a nutrient-dense fish that supports the function of the heart and liver, which are crucial for the production of energy. It's rich in magnesium to support the nervous system, and it can help to reduce the production of stress hormones that cause anxiety and low energy.

It's rich in ...
➔ Omega-3 oils, which balance blood sugar levels and decrease adrenaline and other stress hormones
➔ Selenium, balancing mood and preventing anxiety and depression
➔ The B vitamins, including B_{12}, known as the "energy" vitamin and required for the production of oxygen-carrying red blood cells and the health of the nervous system
➔ Glutathione, which is essential for healthy liver function

Use in ... fish enchiladas or fajitas; pan-fry with garlic, parley, and lemon; roast on skewers with lime and sesame oil; crust with almonds and served on a bed of steamed spinach; prepared as ceviche with mangoes; simmer with potatoes and carrots in a chowder; add to stir-fries and Thai curries.

SEE: HALIBUT WITH MUSTARD & CURRY LEAVES, P. 98; SPICED HALIBUT & OYSTERS WITH BEET SALAD, P. 99

Almonds

✔ Encourage restful sleep
✔ Lift mood
✔ Reduce fatigue
✔ Ease stress
✔ Balance blood sugar levels
✔ Ease digestive problems and constipation
✔ Boost immunity

Almonds are extremely nutritious, with the B vitamins to boost energy and relieve the symptoms of stress. They are high in fiber, helping to balance blood sugar levels and provide a sustained source of energy. They are also rich in magnesium, fighting off muscle fatigue and raising levels of serotonin.

They are rich in ...
➔ Vitamin B_{12}, which boosts energy levels, increases the supply of oxygenated blood, and promotes healthy metabolism
➔ Zinc, which is required for healthy immunity, libido, hormone balance, energy levels, mood, and memory
➔ Calcium and magnesium, easing anxiety and supporting the nervous system
➔ Healthy fats that fight heart disease and balance blood sugar levels

Use in ... almond butter on toast; use almond milk on cereal or in hot drinks; serve chopped almonds in salads with cheese and dried fruit; add to muesli or crumb toppings; coat chicken breasts or fish with ground almonds; use in pesto in place of pine nuts; cook with green lentils, cinnamon, and dried apricots for a delicious stew; add ground almonds to cakes and other baked goods.

SEE: MAPLE-GLAZED GRANOLA WITH FRUIT, P. 38; OATMEAL WITH PRUNE COMPOTE, P. 40; BAKED APPLE & BERRY QUINOA, P. 42

Eggs

✔ Control cravings and addictions
✔ Balance blood sugar levels
✔ Ease mood swings
✔ Provide long-term energy for exercise
✔ Support thyroid function
✔ Boost memory and concentration
✔ Encourage liver health

Eggs contain all eight essential amino acids; these components of proteins have a host of roles in the body, including balancing mood and hormones and providing a sustained source of energy. Eggs contain calcium, iron, zinc, and vitamins A, D, E, and B, making them little powerhouses of nutrition for health on all levels.

They are rich in ...

→ Iodine, encouraging thyroid gland health, promoting healthy metabolism, circulation, and energy levels
→ The B vitamins, for the production of neurotransmitters to regulate mood and conduct nerve messages, and ease irritability, fatigue, and anxiety
→ Choline, boosting memory and energy
→ Sulfur, supporting liver function and, through that, balancing hormones, improving digestion, and raising energy

Use in ... lightly cooked omelets stuffed with spinach and mushrooms; poach and serve with smoked salmon and whole-grain toast; braise in chopped tomatoes and chili for a nutritious Mexican breakfast; hard boil for an energy-boosting snack, particularly during and before exercise; poach and serve on spinach or grilled portabello mushrooms; use in cakes and desserts.

SEE: BAKED APPLE & BERRY QUINOA, P. 42; BAGELS WITH SCRAMBLED EGG & SMOKED SALMON, P. 44; SALMON, DILL & LEEK FRITTATA, P. 48

Chiles

✔ Reduce cravings and addictions
✔ Encourage metabolism
✔ Provide pain relief
✔ Relieve headaches
✔ Promote healthy digestion
✔ Ease constipation and irritable bowel syndrome (IBS)
✔ Boost immunity

The active ingredient in chiles, capsaicin, promotes heart health, easing pain, improving memory and concentration, and even curbing cravings. Chiles and sweet peppers contain substances that increase body heat and blood oxygen levels for at least 20 minutes after eating.

They are rich in ...

→ Capsaicin, which increases the metabolic rate (thus burning calories and providing sustained energy) and relieves and prevent headaches
→ Vitamin C, supporting immunity and reducing the impact of the stress hormone cortisol, which affects both body and mind
→ Vitamin K, aiding a healthy nervous system and brain function
→ Vitamin B_6, good for blood production, a healthy nervous system, and hormone balance

Use in ... meat and vegetarian chili; add to tomato salsas served with whole-grain tortillas; use in cheese and vegetable fajitas and quesadillas; chop into potato salads; stir-fry with red and yellow bell peppers as an accompaniment to grilled tuna.

SEE: CHILE, BEAN & PEPPER SOUP, P. 74; ROASTED VEGETABLE, FETA & BARLEY SALAD, P. 86; TURKEY BURGERS WITH SPICY SALSA, P. 90; CHOCOLATE CHILE DESSERTS, P. 111

Pomegranate

✔ Provides sustained energy
✔ Boosts immunity
✔ Balances weight
✔ Regulates hormones
✔ Balances blood sugar
✔ Encourages healthy digestion
✔ Eases stress

The pomegranate's ruby-red seeds are filled with the energy-producing B vitamins and are a great source of iron, which encourages the production of red blood cells. Research has shown that pomegranate seeds and juice can increase the supply of oxygenated blood to the heart.

It's rich in ...
→ Fiber, balancing hormones and blood sugar levels, promoting digestion, and easing constipation
→ Folic acid, supporting a healthy nervous system and reducing inflammation
→ Flavonoids, which reduce levels of the stress hormone cortisol
→ Phytochemicals that stimulate serotonin and estrogen receptors, improving symptoms of depression, while balancing mood and hormones

Use in ... fresh, fruity salsas served with stews or pork dishes; add to antioxidant-rich smoothies with berries, dates, flaxseeds, and avocado; sprinkle on breakfast cereals, plain yogurt with live cultures and muesli; toss into salad with nuts and feta cheese; stir into couscous with lemon and black pepper; eat as a tasty snack.

SEE: FLAXSEED & POMEGRANATE SMOOTHIE, P. 36; WATERMELON, POMEGRANATE & CHEESE SALAD, P. 84; BUTTERNUT SQUASH STEW WITH HERB QUINOA, P. 96; BRAISED TURKEY WITH YOGURT & POMEGRANATE, P. 109

Salmon

✔ Relieves pain
✔ Encourages memory and concentration
✔ Lifts mood
✔ Enhances energy levels
✔ Promotes relaxation
✔ Aids restful sleep
✔ Reduces growth of candida
✔ Relieves anxiety
✔ Supports thyroid function

Salmon is a great source of omega-3 oils, which are responsible for everything from easing pain and inflammation to encouraging a healthy heart and boosting brain function. It's also full of magnesium, aiding nerve function and promoting sleep.

It's rich in ...
→ Vitamin B_6, which may ease symptoms of PMS, such as anxiety, depression, and breast tenderness, while producing serotonin and supplying oxygenated blood to maintain energy levels
→ Docosahexaenoic acid (DHA), known to reduce depression and improve mood and cognition
→ Vitamin D and certain proteins that reduce the inflammation that causes headaches and other aches and pains
→ Eicosapentaenoic acid, helping to control appetite and preventing unhealthy fat storage

Use in ... pasta dishes and risottos; serve smoked salmon with scrambled or poached eggs for a light lunch or breakfast; top fresh salmon with nutty pesto and put under the broiler; toss flakes of poached salmon into herb salads.

SEE: BAGELS WITH SCRAMBLED EGG & SMOKED SALMON, P. 44; SALMON, DILL & LEEK FRITTATA, P. 48

Butternut squash

✔ Reduces inflammation
✔ Regulates blood sugar levels
✔ Encourages healthy digestion
✔ Promotes relaxation
✔ Lifts mood
✔ Eases pain
✔ Relieves constipation

A great source of fiber, butternut squash can ease digestive complaints and also steady blood sugar levels. The bright color indicates a wealth of antioxidant vitamins and minerals that can help to reduce the impact of stress on your body and mind and prevent inflammatory conditions. The omega-3 oils help your body to convert food and body fat into energy.

It's rich in ...

→ Vitamin B_6, which supports the nervous system, encourages relaxation, and prevents heart disease
→ Vitamin C, helping to balance levels of the stress hormone cortisol, boost immunity, and ease digestion
→ Vitamin D, encouraging the health of your heart and nerves, easing fatigue, and balancing moods
→ Potassium, aiding a healthy nervous system and the relief of pain

Use in ... soups, stews, and curries; mash with crème fraîche and black pepper; roast chunks with onions, ginger, and cinnamon; roast until soft, then blend with ricotta cheese, spinach, basil and garlic for a delicious pasta sauce; stuff ravioli with sage and pureed butternut squash.

SEE: BAKED BARLEY RISOTTO WITH LEEKS,
PEAS & SQUASH, P. 93; BUTTERNUT SQUASH STEW
WITH HERB QUINOA, P. 96

Figs

✔ Encourage brain and nervous system health
✔ Balance blood sugar
✔ Enhance immunity
✔ Reduce inflammation and pain
✔ Balance hormones
✔ Improve liver health
✔ Ease fatigue
✔ Prevent and treat constipation

Figs are an excellent source of fiber, encouraging the health of your digestive system and liver. Their vitamins and minerals ease muscular pain, encourage healthy brain function, and balance blood sugar levels. Dried figs are beneficial, too, but contain fewer nutrients than fresh figs.

They are rich in ...

→ Omega-3 and omega-6 oils, preventing inflammation and related pain, enhancing normal brain function and promoting the release of energy from body fat and food
→ Calcium, required by the body's cells to make energy
→ Potassium, which regulates blood sugar levels, prevents cramping, boosts immunity, and metabolizes carbohydrates and protein for energy
→ Soluble and insoluble fiber, encouraging digestion, balancing blood sugar, and removing toxins to improve liver health

Use in ... fruit cakes and pies; chop (skins on) and add to breakfast cereals and muesli; roast and puree into a compote to serve with yogurt with live cultures; serve with creamy blue cheese and walnuts on a bed of lettuce for a filling salad.

SEE: FIGS WRAPPED IN PROSCUITTO, P. 58;
FIG & WALNUT UPSIDE-DOWN CAKE, P. 125

Beets

✔ Boosts energy levels
✔ Encourages nervous system health
✔ Relaxes and encourages well-being
✔ Supports liver function
✔ Improves exercise performance
✔ Lifts mood
✔ Fights candida
✔ Eases constipation

Beets are naturally high in iron, promoting the production of red blood cells and boosting energy; this plays a role in fighting an overgrowth of candida in the digestive tract, which affects energy levels. High in fiber, it provides a sustained source of energy.

They are rich in ...
→ Folic acid, lifting mood, reducing inflammation, and supporting the nervous system
→ Flavonoids, sulfur, and beta-carotene, stimulating and improving liver function
→ Nitrates, rejuvenating sluggish muscles and improving exercise performance
→ Tryptophan and betain, easing depression, lifting mood, and promoting restful sleep

Use in ... borscht, an Eastern European soup; roast and top with feta cheese and toasted walnuts for a delicious salad; juice and serve on crushed ice for a mood-boosting breakfast or snack; roast and puree with a dash of horseradish and serve with pita bread or crudités; add to stews.

SEE: BAKED BEET CHIPS, P. 55; BEET & APPLE SOUP, P. 72; BUTTERFLIED SARDINES WITH BEET SALSA, P. 80; BEET & ORANGE SALAD, P. 88; BAKED PUMPKIN & GOAT CHEESE, P. 92; SPICED HALIBUT & OYSTERS WITH BEET SALAD, P. 99; BEET BROWNIES, P. 124

Oysters

✔ Boost energy
✔ Support thyroid function
✔ Lift mood
✔ Reduce cravings and addictions
✔ Balance hormones
✔ Ease symptoms of stress
✔ Encourage immunity

Oysters are one of the best sources of zinc, which is essential for athletic performance and strength, balanced hormones, thyroid function, memory, nerve function, and healthy blood sugar levels. They are also rich in easily digested proteins, making them ideal for a quick energy boost.

They are rich in ...
→ Copper and iron, encouraging the production of thyroid hormones and the healthy operation of the thyroid gland
→ Chromium, balancing blood sugar levels and providing sustained energy
→ Selenium, which supports thyroid function, lifts moods, and encourages a healthy heart
→ Zinc, promoting healthy immunity, balanced hormones, protection from stress, and improved energy levels

Use in ... fish casseroles and chowders; grill and serve on whole-grain bread with chives and a little crème fraîche; serve raw in their shells with fresh lemon juice; grill with fennel butter; poach and serve in leek and potato soup.

SEE: SPICED HALIBUT & OYSTERS WITH BEET SALAD, P. 99; CREAMY OYSTER STEW WITH KELP RICE, P. 102

Apricots

✔ Ease muscle tension and headaches
✔ Boost the immune system
✔ Protect against damage caused by stress
✔ Boost energy levels
✔ Balance blood sugar
✔ Encourage the production of red blood cells
✔ Ease constipation
✔ Promote healthy digestion

High in fiber to balance blood sugar levels, support the liver, and promote digestion, apricots are low-GI foods, which can help to stabilize energy levels. They are a good source of vitamin A and potassium and can improve concentration and boost immunity.

They are rich in ...

→ Magnesium, which discourages the release of the stress hormone cortisol and promotes restful sleep
→ Beta-carotene and lycopene, antioxidants to encourage heart health and boost immunity
→ Iron, supporting healthy immunity and improving energy levels
→ Potassium, aiding a healthy nervous system and relief from chronic pain

Use in ... savory and sweet salads, accompanied by crisp apples, goat cheese, and nuts; add to lamb and chicken stews; poach in a little grape juice and puree or serve as a compote with yogurt with live cultures; blend with a frozen banana for an energy-boosting smoothie; eat fresh or dried as a snack; add to whole-grain breads or muffins for extra fiber and nutrition.

SEE: CHERRY, ALMOND & APRICOT BREAKFAST BREAD, P. 43; APRICOT & WALNUT OAT BARS, P. 62

Coconut

✔ Regulates thyroid function
✔ Eases constipation
✔ Raises energy levels
✔ Balances blood sugar
✔ Supports liver function
✔ Increases metabolism
✔ Reduces cravings
✔ Encourages digestion
✔ Fights candida

While coconut contains saturated fats, these particular fats are easily metabolized by the body to provide long-term, sustained energy, while supporting liver function. The oil has been successfully used to combat the growth of candida.

It's rich in ...

→ Medium-chain triglycerides, a form of saturated fat that regulates thyroid function, improves blood sugar balance, promotes heart health, and metabolizes quickly for sustained energy
→ Soluble and insoluble fiber, which reduce blood cholesterol levels, aid digestion, help you feel fuller for longer, and prevent and treat constipation
→ Lauric acid, which boosts metabolism and supports immunity
→ Manganese, aiding the nervous system, thyroid function, and energy production

Use in ... curries and soups; add coconut milk to rice dishes; use shredded dry coconut in muesli and granola; grate fresh coconut into fish and shrimp cakes or whole-grain pancakes; grate fresh coconut over mango slices in a salad with lime and ginger dressing.

SEE: HALIBUT WITH MUSTARD & CURRY LEAVES, P. 98; THAI FRUIT SKEWERS, P. 110; APRICOT & COCONUT PUDDING, P. 116

Flaxseeds

✔ Lift mood
✔ Support liver function
✔ Encourage healthy digestion
✔ Stabilize blood sugar levels
✔ Reduce pain
✔ Fight candida
✔ Balance hormones
✔ Help burn off body fat
✔ Protect against stress

One of the best dietary sources of both fiber and phytoestrogens, flaxseeds are rich in healthy, heart-supporting oils and can encourage efficient digestion, liver function, and blood sugar balance.

They are rich in ...
➔ Omega-3 oils, lifting mood, easing inflammation, encouraging heart and brain health, and preventing surges in stress hormones
➔ Phytoestrogens, balancing hormones and reducing symptoms of PMS and menopause
➔ Magnesium, encouraging the health of the nervous system and promoting restful sleep
➔ Potassium, aiding smooth muscle contraction during exercise, nervous system health, increased alertness, and balanced blood sugar levels

Use in ... smoothies, oatmeal, or yogurt with a little honey; sprinkle over salads and muesli; mix into pancake batter and serve topped with fresh fruit and cottage cheese; make flaxseed and pumpkin muffins for an antioxidant, fiber boost; stir into homemade beef or turkey burgers for nutrients and crunch; add to bread and cakes.

SEE: FLAXSEED & POMEGRANATE SMOOTHIE, P. 36; FLAXSEED & COCOA BITES, P. 61

Seaweeds

✔ Promote thyroid health
✔ Support the adrenal glands
✔ Balance hormones
✔ Boost energy
✔ Encourage metabolism
✔ Regulate blood sugar

All seaweeds, including kelp (kombu and wakame), nori, dulse, arame, and Irish moss, are immensely nutrient-dense sea vegetables with a host of health benefits. They contain dozens of vitamins, minerals, and trace elements and no fewer than 21 amino acids to balance blood sugar and encourage sustained energy levels. They support the glands, in particular the thyroid gland, to promote and balance energy.

They are rich in ...
➔ Iron, boosting energy levels and easing fatigue
➔ Iodine, regulating thyroid and female hormones and encouraging healthy metabolism
➔ Phytoestrogens, which balance hormones and relieve symptoms of PMS and menopause, including bloating, fatigue, and irritability
➔ Fiber and protein, balancing blood sugar levels and supporting health on all levels

Use in ... sushi with fresh salmon or tuna for extra omega oils; sprinkle over food instead of salt; add kelp flakes to stews, casseroles, and soups for extra flavor, nutrients, and texture; eat kelp noodles instead of pasta; add to quiches or frittatas; steam and use as a bed for poached eggs and smoked salmon.

SEE: BROWN RICE & QUINOA SUSHI ROLLS, P. 56; CREAMY OYSTER STEW WITH KELP RICE, P. 102

Turkey

✔ Encourages restful sleep
✔ Reduces anxiety
✔ Lifts mood
✔ Balances blood sugar levels
✔ Encourages a healthy nervous system
✔ Eases depression
✔ Supports the body against stress
✔ Boosts immunity

The amino acids contained in turkey promote both calm and relaxation and are responsible for improving mood and regulating your sleep cycle. Low in saturated fats, it's a healthy alternative to fattier red meats, and the B vitamins it contains help the body to metabolize fats.

It's rich in ...

→ Tryptophan, encouraging the release of the feel-good chemical serotonin that lifts mood and aids sleep
→ Vitamin B$_6$, supporting blood production, a healthy nervous system, and hormone balance
→ Selenium, promoting healthy function of the immune system
→ Zinc, aiding balanced hormones, athletic performance, thyroid health, protection from stress, and improved energy levels

Use in ... stir-fries with ginger, lime, and rice or kelp noodles; sauté with bell peppers and onions and serve in whole-grain wraps as fajitas; grind and mix with lemon zest, tarragon, and chives for turkey burgers; use ground turkey instead of beef in meatballs; use in sandwiches and salads mixed with lemon mayonnaise and crunchy cucumber.

SEE: TURKEY BURGERS WITH SPICY SALSA, P. 90; BRAISED TURKEY WITH YOGURT & POMEGRANATE, P. 109

Barley

✔ Balances blood sugar
✔ Encourages digestion
✔ Boosts energy levels
✔ Encourages balanced weight
✔ Reduces anxiety
✔ Lifts mood
✔ Promotes restful sleep

Barley has the lowest GI rating of all grains, providing a steady supply of energy. It's a good source of fiber to promote healthy digestion and stabilize blood sugar levels, and is full of the B vitamins and selenium, which encourage a healthy nervous system and balanced moods.

It's rich in ...

→ Tryptophan, an amino acid that stimulates the production of feel-good chemical serotonin and encourages restful sleep
→ Copper, which promotes the uptake of iron to boost energy levels
→ Beta-glucan, a chemical that balances blood sugar levels and improves the body's response to glucose
→ Selenium, which helps to balance moods and prevent anxiety and depression

Use in ... barley water with fresh lemon juice to stimulate digestion and encourage calm; bulk out soups, stews, and casseroles with barley to add healthy proteins, slow-release carbohydrates, and flavor; stuff into bell peppers with onions, pine nuts, and feta cheese; add to risottos, pilafs, and desserts instead of rice; use in casseroles, with mushrooms and lima beans.

SEE: BEEF & BARLEY BROTH, P. 79; ROASTED VEGETABLE, FETA & BARLEY SALAD, P. 86, BAKED BARLEY RISOTTO WITH LEEKS, PEAS & SQUASH, P. 93

Yogurt with live active cultures

✔ Reduces stress hormones
✔ Helps ease anxiety and depression
✔ Encourages healthy digestion
✔ Boosts immunity
✔ Promotes relaxation
✔ Improves energy levels
✔ Fights candida
✔ Supports thyroid function

A recent study found that the probiotics (healthy bacteria) in yogurt with live active cultures may alter brain chemistry and can help in the treatment of anxiety and depression-related disorders. Probiotics also encourage healthy digestion and fight candida, promoting higher energy levels.

It's rich in ...

→ Calcium, which can encourage a healthy nervous system as well as restful sleep
→ Probiotics, which improve immunity, enhance digestion, keep candida at bay, and ease symptoms of depression
→ Iodine, which boosts the production of thyroid hormones to encourage healthy energy levels and metabolism
→ Vitamin B_{12}, which is required for the production of oxygen-carrying red blood cells and nervous system health.

Use in ... fruit smoothies to slow down the transit of fruit sugars in the blood; serve with breakfast cereals and muesli instead of milk; mix with lemon zest and fresh herbs as a salad dressing; mix with chives and black pepper to top baked potatoes; blend with a little vanilla sugar as an accompaniment for crisps, cakes, and other baked goods.

SEE: FLAXSEED AND POMEGRANATE SMOOTHIE,
P. 36; FRUITY FROZEN YOGURT, P. 112;
STRAWBERRY & RASPBERRY ROULADE, P. 114

Kidney beans

✔ Balance blood sugar
✔ Promote healthy digestion
✔ Ease anxiety
✔ Reduce symptoms of depression
✔ Encourage the release of serotonin
✔ Raise energy levels
✔ Aid restful sleep
✔ Support liver function
✔ Improve memory and concentration

A rich source of fiber, kidney beans ease constipation and help to keep blood sugar levels stable throughout the day. They are an excellent source of molybdenum, which is required for the liver to perform detoxification.

They are rich in ...

→ Soluble fiber, helping to stabilize blood sugar levels while providing a steady source of energy
→ Iron, which produces the hemoglobin that is necessary for a good supply of oxygenated blood
→ Vitamin B_1, producing energy and regulating cognitive function, including memory
→ Manganese, suprroting energy production and immunity

Use in ... soups, stews, casseroles, and curries; serve cool or warm as a salad with thyme and lemon juice; serve as an accompaniment to fish, curries, and stews; puree with herbs and crème fraîche and serve as a side dish; combine with black and white beans to make a classic three bean salad; include in both meat and vegetarian chilis or in place of beef or turkey in tacos.

SEE: KIDNEY BEAN DIP, P. 54; CHILE, BEAN &
PEPPER SOUP, P. 74

Onions

- ✔ Improve digestion
- ✔ Ease constipation
- ✔ Promote liver health
- ✔ Support the adrenal glands
- ✔ Balance blood sugar levels
- ✔ Boost immunity
- ✔ Promote thyroid function
- ✔ Boost metabolism
- ✔ Attack candida

All members of the onion family (including scallions and leeks) are rich in sulfur and polyphenols, which promote health on many different levels. They have a wealth of cardiovascular benefits, balance blood sugar levels, and are anti-inflammatory, thus easing many types of chronic pain. They are also a good source of prebiotics, which encourage digestive health.

They are rich in ...

- → Chromium, balancing blood sugar levels and providing a sustained source of energy
- → Germanium, which supports immunity and the action of the adrenal and thyroid glands
- → Choline and methionine, which help to prevent fat from being deposited in the liver and protect it from toxins
- → Prebiotics, encouraging healthy digestion, boosting immunity, fighting candida, and easing constipation.

Use in ... soups, stews, casseroles, and curries for flavor and fiber; sauté in olive oil with a little thyme as a side dish; roast and eat whole; use in scrambled eggs and frittatas; roast with potatoes and garlic; stuff inside a chicken with some fresh parsley; add to chopped tomatoes for a fresh salsa or mashed avocado for guacamole; use as a topping for pizza or pasta dishes.

SEE: PIPERADE WITH PASTRAMI, P. 50; KIDNEY BEAN DIP, P. 54; ALL SOUPS, PP. 72–79; WATERMELON, POMEGRANATE & CHEESE SALAD, P. 84; ROASTED VEGETABLE, FETA & BARLEY SALAD, P. 86; BAKED PUMPKIN & GOAT CHEESE, P. 92; BUTTERNUT SQUASH STEW WITH HERB QUINOA, P. 96; HALIBUT WITH MUSTARD & CURRY LEAVES, P. 98; FLOUNDER WITH VEGETABLES PROVENÇAL, P. 100; CHORIZO, CHICKPEA & RED PEPPER STEW, P. 108; BRAISED TURKEY WITH YOGURT & POMEGRANATE, P. 109

WHAT'S YOUR PROBLEM?

Whether you want more energy to improve sporting prowess or simply to stay awake during afternoon meetings, you'll find advice here. These foods have a positive effect on health and work to heal both mind and body. There is an icon by each symptom. These are used throughout the recipe section to highlight which recipes can help combat which symptoms.

Fatigue

Hazelnuts, yogurt with live cultures, sesame seeds, spinach, chickpeas, cocoa, omegranate, figs, eggs, kale, beets, apricots, coconut, olives, cranberries, cinnamon, dates, salmon, halibut, blackberries, onions
Recipes Include:
Flaxseed & cocoa bites, p. 61; Raspberry & coconut smoothie, p. 68; Chickpea, almond & Parmesan pasta, p. 94; Pear & blackberry crisp, p. 117

Anemia

Eggs, beef, chicken, almonds, cocoa, oysters, clams, pumpkin seeds, sesame seeds, sun-dried tomatoes, dried apricots, molasses, spinach, lentils, black beans, brazil nuts, dates, figs, halibut, kidney beans
Recipes Include:
Beef & barley broth, p. 79; Spiced halibut & oysters with beet salad, p. 99; Creamy oyster stew with kelp rice, p. 102; Apricot & coconut pudding, p. 116

Poor concentration

Dark chocolate, oranges, pecans, walnuts, rosemary, avocado, halibut, quinoa, popcorn, blueberries, dairy produce, spinach, squash, potatoes, mango, asparagus, eggs, strawberries, kidney beans, spelt
Recipes Include:
Piperade with pastrami, p. 50; Butternut squash stew with herb quinoa, p. 96; Chocolate chili desserts, p. 111; Perfect pecan pies, p. 120

Sluggishness

Chicken, salmon, eggs, black beans, lentils, walnuts, pineapple, papaya, raspberries, artichokes, rye, butternut squash, rosemary, coconut, beets, quinoa, chiles, asparagus
Recipes Include:
Soft-boiled eggs with asparagus, p. 46; Herbed chicken & ricotta cannelloni, p. 106; Thai fruit skewers, p. 110; Fig & walnut upside-down cake, p. 125

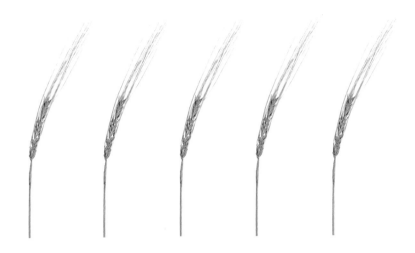

Sleep problems

Turkey, bananas, potatoes, honey, oats, almonds, flaxseeds, sunflower seeds, cherries, tuna, peanuts, cheese, yogurt with live cultures, brown rice, lentils, quinoa, dates, mango, kidney beans, beets
Recipes Include: Cherry, almond & apricot breakfast bread, p. 43; Lemon, pistachio & date squares, p. 64; Braised turkey with yogurt & pomegranate, p. 109

Chronic pain

Salmon, ginger, cherries, olive oil, green tea, walnuts, flaxseeds, soy products, turmeric, grapes, sage, spelt, quinoa, rye, cocoa, brazil nuts, oats, apricots, avocado, bananas, fava beans, garlic, butternut squash, sweet potatoes, chiles, blackberries
Recipes Include: Avocado hummus, p. 52; Butternut squash stew with herb quinoa, p. 96; Apricot & coconut pudding, p. 116

Thyroid imbalance

Seaweeds, turkey, cocoa, shrimp, beef, oysters, cashews, sunflower seeds, raspberries, red peppers, tomatoes, coconut, brazil nuts, eggs, oats, yogurt with live cultures, chicken, haddock, maple syrup, pumpkin, squash, kiwifruit, onions
Recipes Include: Salmon, dill & leek frittata, p. 48; Baked barley risotto with leeks, peas & squash, p. 93; Creamy oyster stew with kelp rice, p. 102

Congested liver

Cabbage, kale, garlic, beets, carrots, green tea, spinach, endive, avocado, apples, olive oil, lemons, walnuts, turmeric, onions, eggs, pears, pine nuts, almonds, peanuts, cauliflower, cider vinegar, papaya, halibut, blackberries, rosemary, kidney beans, figs, tuna
Recipes Include: Creamy kale, white bean & rosemary soup, p. 76; Honey-glazed tuna with parsnip puree, p. 103

Anxiety

Peaches, blueberries, almonds, oats, dark chocolate, salmon, broccoli, brown rice, seaweeds, milk, turkey, melon, beef, peanuts, soy products, grapefruit, cherries, Romaine lettuce, barley, halibut, kidney beans, beets, tuna

Recipes Include:
Lemon, pistachio & date squares, p. 64; Florentines, p. 66; Roasted vegetable, feta & barley salad, p. 86; Beet brownies, p. 124

Addictions

Kale, cabbage, Romaine lettuce, beets, carrots, berries, grapefruit, ginger, eggs, brazil nuts, turkey, dark chocolate, peppermint, mackerel, cod, chickpeas, rye, strawberries, chiles

Recipes Include:
Beet & orange salad, p. 88; Chorizo, chickpea & red pepper stew, p. 108; Chocolate chili desserts, p. 111; Strawberry & raspberry roulade, p. 114

Poor adrenal function

Flaxseeds, olive oil, butternut squash, pumpkin, papaya, red bell peppers, tomatoes, salmon, mackerel, kiwifruit, cherries, onions, garlic, coconut, sesame seeds, sunflower seeds, kale, eggs, brown rice, broccoli, halibut, chiles, avocado, tuna, onions, mango

Recipes Include:
Baked pumpkin & goat cheese, p. 92; Apricot & coconut pudding, p. 116

Fluctuating blood sugar

Figs, almonds, quinoa, millet, avocado, walnuts, lentils, popcorn, cocoa, peanuts, oats, apples, sweet potatoes, eggs, grapefruit, raspberries, watermelon, sunflower seeds, turmeric, asparagus, strawberries, halibut, blackberries, kidney beans, tuna, onions

Recipes Include:
Kidney bean dip, p.54; Smoked chicken with beans, walnuts & tarragon, p. 83

Candida

Yogurt with live cultures, seaweeds, kale, cider vinegar, onions, radishes, avocado, cabbage, celery, peas, barley, brown rice, wild rice, pumpkin seeds, sesame seeds, soy products, ginger, brazil nuts, almonds, chicken, chickpeas, black-eyed peas, kidney beans

Recipes Include: Smoked chicken with beans, walnuts & tarragon, p. 83; Baked barley risotto with leeks, peas & squash, p. 93

Constipation

Strawberries, figs, barley, whole wheat, yogurt with live cultures, papaya, broccoli, brown rice, carrots, sweet potatoes, berries, oats, parsnips, dates, artichokes, black beans, rye, salmon, apricots, kidney beans, blackberries, beets, prunes, onions, flaxseeds

Recipes Include: Flaxseed & pomegranate smoothie, p. 36; Italian tomato & bean soup, p. 78; Fruity frozen yogurt, p. 112

Hormonal swings

Flaxseeds, broccoli, kale, soy products, quinoa, buckwheat, rice, coconut, oranges, turkey, walnuts, green tea, tomatoes, spinach, carrots, eggs, lentils, figs brown rye, oats, watermelon, papaya, chickpeas, sardines, pumpkin, peaches, prunes

Recipes Include: Hearty kale soup with garlic croutons, p. 75; Turkey burgers with spicy salsa, p. 90; Butternut squash stew with herb quinoa, p. 96

Energy for exercise

Beets, coconut, watercress, millet, quinoa, almonds, bananas, salmon, black beans, lentils, chickpeas, carrots, blackberries, raspberries, eggs, blueberries, red bell peppers, walnuts, mango, watermelon, rosemary, apricots

Recipes Include: Roasted peppers with tapenade, p. 82; Salmon with horseradish crust, p. 104

PUTTING IT
ALL TOGETHER

Meal Planner	Monday	Tuesday	Wednesday
Breakfast	Maple-glazed granola with fruit, p. 38	Flaxseed & pomegranate smoothie, p36	Soft-boiled eggs with asparagus, p. 46
Morning snack	Brown rice & quinoa sushi rolls, p. 56	5 dried apricots	Lemon, pistachio & date squares, p. 64
Lunch	Smoked chicken with beans, walnuts & tarragon, p. 83	Beef & barley broth, p. 79	Beet & orange salad, p. 88
Afternoon snack	Baked beet chips, p. 55	Avocado hummus, p. 52, with pita bread	Kidney bean dip, p. 54, with rice cakes
Dinner	Halibut with mustard & curry leaves, p. 98	Chickpea, almond & Parmesan pasta, p. 94	Turkey burgers with spicy salsa, p. 90
Dessert	Thai fruit skewers, p. 110	Beet brownies, p. 124	Strawberry & raspberry roulade, p. 114

WEEK 1

Thursday	Friday	Saturday	Sunday
Blackberry breakfast bars, p. 39	Oatmeal with prune compote, p. 40	Bagels with scrambled egg & smoked salmon, p. 44	Smoked ham & cherry tomato omelet, p. 49
Flaxseed & cocoa bites, p. 61	Apricot & walnut oat bars, p. 62	Tropical fruit smoothie, p. 70	Raspberry & coconut smoothie, p. 68
Italian tomato & bean soup, p. 78	Watermelon, pomegranate & cheese salad, p. 84	Roasted vegetable, feta & barley salad, p. 86	Hearty kale soup with garlic croutons, p. 75
Florentines, p. 66	Figs wrapped in proscuitto, p. 58	Popcorn	Cocoa & cinnamon-covered almonds, p. 60
Spiced halibut & oysters with beet salad, p. 99	Chorizo, chickpea & red pepper stew, p. 108	Flounder with vegetables provençal, p. 100	Baked pumpkin & goat cheese, p. 92
Pear & blackberry crisp, p. 117	Fruity frozen yogurt, p. 112	Fig & walnut upside-down cake, p. 125	Apricot & coconut pudding, p. 116

Meal Planner	Monday	Tuesday	Wednesday
Breakfast	Baked apple & berry quinoa, p. 42	Soft-boiled eggs with asparagus, p. 46	Blackberry breakfast bars, p. 39
Morning snack	5 dried apricots	Kidney bean dip, p. 54, on rye toast	Cocoa & cinnamon-covered almonds, p. 60
Lunch	Chili, bean & bell pepper soup, p. 74	Watermelon, pomegranate & cheese salad, p. 84	Beet & apple soup, p. 72
Afternoon snack	Avocado hummus, p. 52, with crudités	Florentines, p. 66	Popcorn
Dinner	Braised turkey with yogurt & pomegranate, p. 109	Honey-glazed tuna with parsnip puree, p. 103	Butternut squash stew with herb quinoa, p. 96
Dessert	Orange, rhubarb & ginger slump, p. 122	Pear & blackberry crisp, p. 117	Strawberry & raspberry roulade, p. 114

WEEK 2

Thursday	Friday	Saturday	Sunday
Cherry, almond & apricot breakfast bread, p. 43	Oatmeal with prune compote, p. 40	Piperade with pastrami, p. 50	Salmon, dill & leek frittata, p. 48
Baked beet chips, p. 55	Flaxseed & cocoa bites, p. 61	Raspberry & coconut smoothie, p. 68	Apricot & walnut oat bars, p. 62
Roasted peppers with tapenade, p. 82	Butterflied sardines with beet salsa, p. 80	Roasted vegetable, feta & barley salad, p. 86	Creamy kale, white bean & rosemary soup, p. 76
Tropical fruit smoothie, p. 70	Brown rice & quinoa sushi rolls, p. 56	Lemon, pistachio & date squares, p. 64	Figs wrapped in proscuitto, p. 58
Salmon with horseradish crust, p. 104	Herbed chicken & ricotta cannelloni, p. 106	Creamy oyster stew with kelp rice, p. 102	Baked barley risotto with leeks, peas & squash, p. 93
Hot blackberry & apple trifle, p. 118	Perfect pecan pies, p. 120	Chocolate chile desserts, p. 111	Fruity frozen yogurt, p. 112

ENERGY
RECIPES

FLAXSEED & POMEGRANATE SMOOTHIE

Bursting with antioxidants and omega-3 oils, this delicious fiber-rich breakfast is ideal when you are short on time.

Preparation time: 10 minutes
Serves 4
....

3 tablespoons ground **flaxseeds**
1 cup **frozen strawberries**
1 cup **frozen apricot chunks**
seeds from 2 **pomegranates**
1 cup **plain yogurt with live active cultures**
2 tablespoons **honey**

Place all the ingredients in a blender or food processor and blend until smooth. Pour into tall glasses and serve immediately.

....

MAPLE-GLAZED GRANOLA WITH FRUIT

A satisfying multinutrient breakfast in a bowl, with oodles of antioxidants, omega-3 oils, and slow-release energy.

Preparation time: 10 minutes, plus cooling
Cooking time: 5–8 minutes
Serves 4
....

2 tablespoons **olive oil**
2 tablespoons **maple syrup**
⅓ cup **slivered almonds**
⅓ cup **pine nuts**
3 tablespoons **sunflower seeds**
¼ cup **rolled oats**
1⅔ cup **plain yogurt with live active cultures**, to serve

Fruit salad
1 **mango**, pitted, peeled, and sliced
2 **kiwifruit**, peeled and sliced
small bunch of **red seedless grapes**, halved
finely grated zest and juice of 1 **lime**

Heat the oil in an ovenproof skillet over medium heat, add the maple syrup, nuts, seeds, and oats, and toss together. Place in a preheated oven, at 350°F, for 5–8 minutes, stirring once, until evenly toasted. Let cool.

....

To make the fruit salad, mix together all the ingredients in a large bowl. Divide among 4 serving dishes and top with the yogurt and granola. Serve immediately.

....

Store any leftover granola in an airtight container for up to 10 days.

....

BLACKBERRY BREAKFAST BARS

These chewy, blackberry-filled bars are loaded with slow-release carbs and fiber to set you up for the day.

Preparation time: 15 minutes
Cooking time: 50 minutes
Makes 16
....

1 cup **whole-wheat flour**
1 cup **rolled oats**
½ cup packed **light brown sugar**
1 teaspoon **ground cinnamon**, plus
   extra for dusting
¼ teaspoon **baking soda**
1 stick **butter**, melted

Filling
2 cups **blackberries**,
   defrosted if frozen
2 tablespoons **sugar**
2 tablespoons **water**
finely grated zest and juice of ½ **lemon**
1 teaspoon **ground cinnamon**

Put all the filling ingredients into a large saucepan over medium heat and bring to a boil. Reduce the heat and simmer for about 10 minutes, stirring regularly, until the blackberries are breaking down and taking on a saucelike appearance. Remove from the heat and set aside.
....

Put the flour, oats, brown sugar, cinnamon, and baking soda into a medium bowl. Add the butter and stir until well combined.
....

Press half the oat mixture into an even layer in a greased 8 inch square baking pan and place in a preheated oven, at 350°F, for 20 minutes.
....

Let cool slightly, then spread the blackberry filling evenly over the top of the crust. Sprinkle over the remaining oat mixture and use your hands to gently press it into the filling.
....

Return to the oven for another 20 minutes, until the topping is golden. Let cool, then cut into 16 bars to serve.
....

OATMEAL WITH PRUNE COMPOTE

This tasty breakfast will speed up the digestion and lift energy levels too. Use dried figs instead of prunes, if you prefer.

Preparation time: 5 minutes
Cooking time: about 20 minutes
Serves 4

4 cups **milk** or **soy milk**
2 cups **water**
1 teaspoon **vanilla extract**
pinch of **ground cinnamon**
pinch of **salt**
2 cups **rolled oats**
3 tablespoons **slivered almonds**, toasted

Compote
2 cups **dried prunes**
½ cup **apple juice**
1 small **cinnamon stick**
1 **clove**
1 tablespoon mild **agave nectar**
    or **honey**
1 unpeeled **orange**, quartered

To make the compote, put all the ingredients into a small saucepan over medium heat and bring to a boil. Reduce the heat and simmer gently for 10–12 minutes or until softened and slightly sticky. Let cool, then chill in the refrigerator until ready to serve.

Place the milk, measured water, vanilla, cinnamon, and salt in a large saucepan over medium heat and bring slowly to a boil. Stir in the oats, then reduce the heat and simmer gently, stirring occasionally, for 8–10 minutes, until creamy and tender. Spoon the oatmeal into serving bowls, sprinkle with the almonds, and serve with the prune compote.

BAKED APPLE & BERRY QUINOA

This fiber-rich, moist breakfast bake provides a wealth of nutrients to balance blood sugar and jump-start the digestion.

Preparation time: 20 minutes
Cooking time: 1 hour
Serves 4
················

1 cup **quinoa**
2 teaspoons **ground cinnamon**
1 teaspoon **grated nutmeg**
¼ teaspoon **ground cloves**
2 cups **frozen mixed berries**,
    such as blueberries, blackberries,
    and raspberries
2 **apples**, cored and chopped
2 extra-large **eggs**, lightly beaten
2 cups **milk** or **soy milk**
¼ cup **maple syrup**
½ cup chopped **walnut pieces**
½ cup chopped **almonds**
**plain yogurt with live active
    cultures**, to serve

Put the quinoa into a large bowl with the cinnamon, nutmeg, and cloves and mix until well combined. Spread out in the bottom of a lightly greased 8 inch square baking pan and sprinkle with the berries and apples.
····································

Whisk together the eggs, milk, and maple syrup and pour the mixture over the quinoa and fruit mixture. Sprinkle the nuts evenly on top.
····································

Place in a preheated oven, at 350°F, for 1 hour, until the quinoa has absorbed almost all of the liquid. Serve warm with a little yogurt.
····································

CHERRY, ALMOND & APRICOT BREAKFAST BREAD

Dried fruit and nuts add fiber to this nutrient-rich breakfast loaf and provide a boost of energy.

Preparation time: 15 minutes, plus standing
Cooking time: 50 minutes
Makes 1 large loaf

....

½ cup **rolled oats**
1 cup **dried sour cherries**
½ cup chopped **dried apricots**
2 tablespoons **ground almonds**
1¼ cups **milk** or **soy milk**
⅓ cup firmly packed **light brown sugar**
3 tablespoons **maple syrup**
1 extra-large **egg**, beaten
2 cups **whole-wheat flour**
2 teaspoons **ground cinnamon**
1 tablespoon **baking powder**
½ cup chopped **almonds**

Put the oats into a large bowl with the cherries, apricots, and ground almonds. Put the milk into a small saucepan over medium heat until hot, then pour it over the oat mixture and stir well. Let stand for 10 minutes.

....

Add the sugar, maple syrup, and egg to the oat mixture and mix to combine.

....

Sift the flour, cinnamon, and baking powder into a separate bowl, mix well, then fold into the oat mixture, a little at a time, until well combined. Stir in half the almonds and transfer the mixture to a lightly greased, large loaf pan. Sprinkle the remaining almonds on top.

....

Place in a preheated oven, at 350°F, for 45 minutes, until lightly browned and risen, and a toothpick inserted into the center comes out clean.

....

Turn out onto a wire rack and serve warm or cold, toasted if desired. Store any leftover bread in an airtight container for up to a week.

....

BAGELS WITH SCRAMBLED EGG & SMOKED SALMON

This high-protein breakfast will fill you and give you plenty of energy for whatever the morning brings.

Preparation time: 10 minutes
Cooking time: 12–15 minutes
Serves 4
....

4 **hot-smoked salmon fillets**,
    about 4 oz each
8 **eggs**
½ cup **milk** or **soy milk**
1 tablespoon chopped **chervil**
1 tablespoon chopped **chives**,
    plus extra to garnish
2 tablespoons **butter**
4 **whole-wheat bagels**, halved
⅓ cup **cream cheese**
finely grated zest and juice of 1 **lemon**
sea salt and **black pepper**

Arrange the smoked salmon on an aluminum foil-lined baking sheet, cover with more foil, and place in a preheated oven, at 350°F, for 12–15 minutes or until heated through.
....

Meanwhile, break the eggs into a bowl with the milk and herbs, season to taste, and beat lightly. Melt the butter in a large, nonstick saucepan over medium-low heat until frothy, then pour in the egg mixture. Reduce the heat and stir the eggs gently for 5–6 minutes or until creamy and beginning to set.
....

Toast the bagels and spread with the cream cheese, then sprinkle with the lemon zest and juice. Arrange half a bagel on each serving plate, cut side up, and spoon the scrambled egg on top.
....

Flake the salmon over the scrambled egg and serve immediately, garnished with chives and black pepper and each topped with a remaining bagel half.
....

SOFT-BOILED EGGS
WITH ASPARAGUS

A simple yet hugely nutritious breakfast to lift the mood, boost energy, balance blood sugar, and enhance concentration.

Preparation time: 5 minutes
Cooking time: 5 minutes
Serves 4
....

1 pound **asparagus**, trimmed
8 **eggs**
pinch of **paprika**
sea salt

Cook the asparagus in a steamer set over a saucepan of gently simmering water for about 5 minutes, or until tender with just a little bite.
....

Meanwhile, bring a saucepan of water to a boil, gently add the eggs, and cook for 4 minutes or until soft-boiled. Remove from the pan and place in egg cups.
....

Slice the tops off the eggs and sprinkle a little salt and paprika inside. Serve immediately with the asparagus spears for dipping.
....

SALMON, DILL & LEEK FRITTATA

Combining salmon and eggs for breakfast is a sure way to get the day off to a good start. You'll be bursting with energy!

Preparation time: 10 minutes
Cooking time: 35 minutes
Serves 4
....

1 tablespoon **olive oil**
2 large **leeks**, trimmed, cleaned and finely sliced
5 oz **smoked salmon**, cut into strips
8 **eggs**
1 teaspoon grated **nutmeg**
¼ cup finely chopped **dill**
sea salt and **black pepper**

Heat the olive oil in a saucepan over medium heat, add the leeks, and cook for about 10 minutes, until soft. Spread over the bottom of a lightly greased 8–9 inch tart pan and sprinkle with the smoked salmon.
....

Break the eggs into a bowl with the nutmeg and dill, season to taste, and beat lightly. Pour the egg mixture over the salmon and leeks and place in a preheated oven, at 375°F, for 25 minutes or until golden and firm to the touch. Serve hot or cold.
....

SMOKED HAM & CHERRY TOMATO OMELET

Omelets make a great energy-boosting breakfast, and the fresh herbs add extra flavor and nutrients.

Preparation time: 10 minutes
Cooking time: about 20 minutes
Serves 4
....

4 teaspoons extra virgin **canola oil**
4 **shallots**, thinly sliced
8 **eggs**
2 tablespoons chopped **mixed herbs**, such as chives, chervil, parsley, basil, and thyme
12 **cherry tomatoes**, halved
5 oz **smoked ham**, thinly sliced
sea salt and **black pepper**

Heat 1 teaspoon of the oil in a skillet over medium-low heat. Add the shallots and cook gently for 4–5 minutes, until softened. Meanwhile, break the eggs into a bowl with the herbs, season to taste, and beat lightly.
....

Remove three-quarters of the shallots from the skillet with a slotted spoon and set aside in a bowl. Pour one-quarter of the egg mixture into the skillet and sprinkle with one-quarter of the tomatoes. Cook, stirring gently, until the egg is almost set.
....

Sprinkle one-quarter of the ham evenly over the top of the omelettand cook gently for another minute. Fold the omelet in half and transfer to a warm serving plate.
....

Use the remaining ingredients to make 3 more omelets in the same way and serve immediately.
....

PIPERADE WITH PASTRAMI

Immune-boosting bell peppers and garlic combine with protein-rich pastrami and eggs for a high-flavor, high-energy meal.

Preparation time: 25 minutes
Cooking time: 30 minutes
Serves 4
....

3 small **bell peppers** in mixed colors
2 tablespoons **olive oil**
1 **onion**, finely chopped
4 **tomatoes**, peeled
2 **garlic cloves**, crushed
4 extra-large **eggs**
1 teaspoon chopped **thyme**,
   plus extra to garnish
4 oz **pastrami,** thinly sliced
sea salt and **black pepper**

Place the bell peppers under a preheated hot broiler for about 10 minutes, turning regularly, until blistered and blackened all over. Rub off the skins and rinse the peppers under cold running water. Halve, seed, and core the bell peppers and cut the flesh into strips.

....

Heat half the oil in a large skillet over medium-low heat, add the onion, and cook gently for 10 minutes, until softened and transparent.

....

Meanwhile, seed the tomatoes and chop the flesh. Add the garlic, tomatoes, and bell peppers to the skillet and simmer for 5 minutes, until any juice has evaporated from the tomatoes. Set aside until ready to serve.

....

Break the eggs into a bowl with the thyme, season to taste, and beat lightly. Heat the remaining oil in a saucepan over medium heat, add the eggs, and cook for about 5 minutes, until lightly scrambled.

....

Stir the eggs into the bell pepper mixture, reheated if necessary. Arrange the pastrami on the serving plates and spoon the eggs over. Serve immediately, garnished with a little extra thyme.

....

AVOCADO HUMMUS

The chickpeas in this creamy hummus balance blood sugar and boost energy; the avocado cleanses, soothes, and nourishes.

Preparation time: 10 minutes, plus chilling
Serves 4
....

1 large ripe **avocado**, peeled and pitted
1 (15 oz) can **chickpeas**, rinsed
    and drained
1 **garlic clove**, crushed
finely grated zest and juice
    of 2 **lemons**
1 small **red chile**, seeded and
    finely chopped
1 teaspoon **ground cumin**
sea salt
whole-wheat pita breads
    or **crudités**, to serve

Put all the ingredients into a blender or food processor and blend until smooth. Transfer to a serving bowl and chill in the refrigerator for at least 1 hour. Serve with toasted pita breads or crudités.
....

KIDNEY BEAN DIP

This hearty, nourishing dip is guaranteed to provide energy.
Serve as a snack or an accompaniment to a Mexican meal.

Preparation time: 15 minutes
Cooking time: 10 minutes
Serves 4
....

1 tablespoon **olive oil**
1 **onion**, chopped
1 **garlic clove**, chopped
1 small **red chile**, seeded and
   finely chopped
¾ cup canned **diced tomatoes**
1 (15 oz) can **kidney beans**,
   rinsed and drained
finely grated zest and juice of 1 **lime**
½ cup **cream cheese**
sea salt and **black pepper**
whole-wheat soft flour **tortillas**,
   toasted, to serve

Heat the olive oil in a skillet over medium
heat, add the onion, and cook for
2–3 minutes, until beginning to soften.
....

Add the garlic and chile and cook for
1 minute, then add the tomatoes and
beans and cook for another 3 minutes.
....

Transfer to a blender or food processor
with the lime zest and lime juice and
blend until smooth. Add the cream
cheese and blend again to combine.
....

Season to taste, transfer to a serving
bowl, and serve warm or cold with
toasted tortillas, cut into triangles.
....

BAKED BEET CHIPS

A colorful, antioxidant-rich snack, it is full of fiber and nutrients that support the nervous system and liver and lift the mood and energy levels.

Preparation time: 10 minutes, plus cooling
Cooking time: 1 hour
Serves 4
....

4 **beets**, peeled and finely sliced
2 tablespoons **olive oil**
sea salt and **black pepper**

Put the beets into a bowl with the olive oil and 1 teaspoon salt, and toss to coat. Spread out in a single layer on 2 baking sheets lined with nonstick parchment paper.
....

Place in a preheated oven, at 275°F, for 30 minutes, then rotate the sheets so the chips cook evenly.
....

Cook for another 30 minutes, until dry and crispy. Sprinkle with a little more sea salt and a good grinding of black pepper and let cool.
....

BROWN RICE & QUINOA SUSHI ROLLS

These tasty snacks support the thyroid, balance blood sugar, and boost energy. Freeze leftover brown rice and quinoa to make preparation quicker next time.

Preparation time: 20 minutes, plus cooling
Cooking time: 30 minutes
Serves 4
....

½ cup **short-grain brown rice**
⅔ cup **quinoa**
2 tablespoons **rice vinegar**
1 tablespoon **cider vinegar**
2 tablespoons **sugar**
½ teaspoon **sea salt**
oil, for greasing
4 sheets of **nori seaweed**
1 small unpeeled **carrot**, shredded
½ **cucumber**, cut into matchsticks
1 large **avocado**, peeled, pitted,
    and cut into matchsticks
1 tablespoon **toasted sesame seeds**
soy sauce, to serve

Cook the brown rice and quinoa in 2 separate saucepans of lightly salted boiling water according to package directions, then drain and mix together in a large bowl.

....

Meanwhile, place the vinegars in a small bowl with the sugar and salt and whisk until dissolved. Pour it over the hot rice mixture, toss to combine, season to taste, and let cool.

....

Lightly grease a large square of plastic wrap and place a sheet of seaweed on top. Arrange one-quarter of the rice mixture in a line down the middle of the sheet of seaweed and top with some carrot, cucumber, avocado, and sesame seeds.

....

Lift the edge of the plastic wrap and use it to roll one side of the nori over the filling, and keep rolling to enclose the filling in the seaweed and create a neat roll. Wet the edge of the seaweed to seal the roll, if necessary.

....

Repeat to make 4 sushi rolls, then slice each into 6 pieces, using a sharp knife. Chill in the refrigerator until ready to serve, accompanied by a bowl of soy sauce for dipping.

....

FIGS WRAPPED IN PROSCUITTO

Rich in fiber to aid digestion and balance blood sugar, this snack also works well on a bed of arugula as an elegant appetizer.

Preparation time: 10 minutes
Cooking time: 10 minutes
Serves 4
················

1 tablespoon **honey**
1 tablespoon **balsamic vinegar**
1 tablespoon **olive oil**
4 **figs**, stems removed, halved lengthwise
2 slices of **proscuitto**
sea salt and **black pepper**

Put the honey into a small bowl with the vinegar and olive oil, and season to taste. Brush the mixture over the fig halves. Cut each slice of proscuitto into 4 strips and wrap a strip around each of the pieces of fig.
····························

Arrange on a baking sheet lined with nonstick parchment paper and place in a preheated oven, at 350°F, for 10 minutes, until the proscuitto begins to color.
····························

Transfer to serving plates, drizzle any juices over the top, and serve warm or cold.
····························

COCOA & CINNAMON-COVERED ALMONDS

This tasty snack provides sustained energy and health-boosting omega oils. It also supports the thyroid gland and eases pain.

Preparation time: 10 minutes
Cooking time: 15 minutes
Serves 4-6
·················

⅓ cup **honey**
1 teaspoon **sea salt**
1 cup **almonds**
olive oil, for brushing
2 tablespoons unsweetened **cocoa powder**
2 teaspoons **ground cinnamon**

Put the honey and salt into a saucepan over medium heat and cook until the salt has dissolved and the mixture is warm. Add the almonds and stir until they are coated.
···

Spread them out on a baking sheet lined with nonstick parchment paper brushed with oil. Place in a preheated oven, at 350°F, for 10 minutes, until golden, stirring frequently. Let cool for about 5 minutes.
···

Put the cocoa powder and cinnamon into a freezer bag and add the warm almonds. Shake the bag until the almonds are completely covered, then transfer to a plate and let cool. Store any leftover almonds in an airtight container for up to 2 weeks.
·····················

FLAXSEED & COCOA BITES

Easy to prepare, these delicious little balls will satisfy hunger and provide a boost of omega oils and fiber to keep you going.

Preparation time: 15 minutes, plus soaking and chilling
Makes 12
....

1 cup **pitted dried dates**
½ cup **almonds**
½ cp **walnut pieces**
⅓ cup unsweetened **dry coconut**
¼ cup unsweetened **cocoa powder**
1 tablespoon **flaxseeds**

Soak the dates in a little warm water for about 10 minutes, until plump.
....

Put the almonds, walnuts, coconut, cocoa, and flaxseeds into a blender or food processor and blend until smooth. Add the dates, one by one, with the motor running, and blend until the mixture is moist and smooth, adding a little of the date soaking water if it isn't holding together.
....

Divide the mixture into 12 portions and use your hands to shape into balls. Chill in the refrigerator for 10–15 minutes before serving.
....

APRICOT & WALNUT OAT BARS

With fiber, omega oils, antioxidants, and plenty of soothing oats, these oat bars are bound to be popular.

Preparation time: 10 minutes
Cooking time: 20 minutes
Makes 16
....

1¼ sticks **butter**
⅓ cup **honey**
⅓ cup firmly packed **dark brown sugar**
2¾ cups **rolled oats**
8 soft **dried apricots**, chopped
¾ cup chopped **walnut pieces**

Put the butter, honey, and sugar into a large saucepan over medium heat until melted. Add the oats, apricots, and walnuts and stir until well combined.
....

Press the mixture in an even layer in an 8 inch square baking pan lined with nonstick parchment paper and place in a preheated oven, at 350°F, for 15 minutes, until golden. Let cool, then cut into squares before serving.
....

LEMON, PISTACHIO & DATE SQUARES

Rich in fiber, aiding digestion and balancing blood sugar, and the B vitamins, which support the nervous system, these crunchy bars are delicious.

Preparation time: 10 minutes, plus cooling and chilling
Cooking time: 20 minutes
Makes 15–20

....

finely grated zest of 1 **lemon**
3 **dried dates**, chopped
½ cup **unsalted pistachios**, chopped
¾ cup **slivered almonds**, chopped
½ cup **light brown sugar**
4 cups **millet flakes**
¾ cup **oat flakes**
1 (15 oz) can **condensed milk**
3 tablespoons **mixed seeds**,
    such as pumpkin and sunflower

Put all the ingredients into a large bowl and mix until well combined. Spoon into an 11 x 7 inch baking pan lined with nonstick parchment paper and place in a preheated oven, at 350°F, for 20 minutes.

....

Let cool in the pan, then mark into 15–20 squares and chill in the refrigerator until firm.

....

FLORENTINES

A nutty little treat, loaded with fiber- and iron-rich dried fruits and mood-lifting dark chocolate.

Preparation time: 25 minutes, plus cooling and setting
Cooking time: 25–30 minutes
Makes 48

·················

1¼ sticks **butter**
¾ cup plus 2 tablespoons **sugar**
¼ cup **heavy cream**
½ cup **candied peel**, chopped
⅓ cup **dried cherries**, chopped
½ cup **slivered almonds**
¼ cup **dried cranberries**
3 tablespoons **pine nuts**
⅓ cup **whole-wheat flour**
5 oz **semisweet dark chocolate**
5 oz **white chocolate**

Put the butter and sugar into a saucepan over low heat until the butter has melted. Increase the heat and bring to a boil. Immediately remove the pan from the heat and add the cream, candied peel, cherries, almonds, cranberries, pine nuts, and flour. Stir well until evenly combined.

···

Arrange heaping teaspoonfuls of half the dough on 2 baking sheets lined with nonstick parchment paper, leaving a 2 inch gap between them for spreading. Bake in a preheated oven, at 350°F, for 7 minutes.

···

Use a 3 inch cookie cutter to drag the edges of the cookies into neat circles about 2 inches across, then return to the oven for another 3–4 minutes, until golden around the edges.

···

Let cool on the baking sheets for 2 minutes, then transfer the cookies to a tray lined with parchment paper and let cool completely. Repeat with the remaining mixture.

···

Melt the chocolates in 2 separate heatproof bowls set over saucepans of simmering water. Drizzle the melted chocolate over the cookies and let set.

···

RASPBERRY & COCONUT SMOOTHIE

This creamy smoothie will satisfy even the sweetest tooth. Coconut aids thyroid and liver function and raspberries provide a good hit of fiber.

Preparation time: 5 minutes
Serves 4
....

3½ cups **coconut milk**
1⅔ cups **frozen raspberries**
1 teaspoon **ground cinnamon**
1 teaspoon **vanilla extract**
3 tablespoons **maple syrup**

Put all the ingredients into a blender or food processor and blend until smooth, adding a little water if it is too thick. Serve immediately.
....

TROPICAL FRUIT SMOOTHIE

For a little liquid energy, try this refreshing smoothie to jump-start the digestion and banish that heavy, sluggish feeling.

Preparation time: 10 minutes, plus freezing
Serves 4
....

1 large **banana**, peeled and sliced
1 large ripe **mango**, peeled, pitted, and coarsely chopped
⅔ cup **plain yogurt with live active cultures**
1¼ cups **pineapple juice**
pineapple chunks, to decorate (optional)

Put the banana pieces into a freezerproof container and freeze for at least 2 hours or overnight.
....

Put the frozen banana into blender or food processor with the mango, yogurt, and pineapple juice and blend until smooth. Serve immediately, with pineapple chunks to decorate, if desired.
....

BEET & APPLE SOUP

This light but filling soup will improve the digestion, support the liver, and provide a hit of energy-boosting nitrates.

Preparation time: 20 minutes
Cooking time: 40 minutes
Serves 4
....

6 **beets**, peeled and chopped
2 tablespoons **olive oil**
2 teaspoons **dried thyme**
2 teaspoons **cumin seeds**
1 tablespoon **butter**
1 large **onion**, finely chopped
1 large **sweet, crisp apple**, peeled, cored, and chopped
1 **Granny Smith** or other **cooking apple**, peeled, cored, and chopped
6 cups **vegetable stock**
sea salt and **black pepper**
Greek yogurt with live active cultures, to serve

Put the beets into a large bowl with the olive oil, thyme, and cumin seeds, season to taste, and toss together. Transfer to a baking sheet and place in a preheated oven, at 400°F, for 30 minutes, until the beets are tender.
....

Meanwhile, melt the butter in a large saucepan over medium heat and add the onion. Cook for 5 minutes, stirring frequently, until softened. Add the apple and cook for another 5 minutes.
....

Add the beets and any juices to the pan along with the stock, bring to a boil, and cook for 10 minutes. Let cool slightly.
....

Place the soup in a blender or food processor, in batches if necessary, and blend until smooth. Season to taste and reheat if desired. Serve hot or cold, with a swirl of yogurt in the top of each bowl.
....

CHILE, BEAN & BELL PEPPER SOUP

Rich in antioxidants, fiber, and the B vitamins, this is an essential soup for anyone low in energy.

Preparation time: 20 minutes
Cooking time: 35 minutes
Serves 4

2 tablespoons **sunflower oil**
1 large **onion**, finely chopped
4 **garlic cloves**, finely chopped
2 **red bell peppers**, cored, seeded, and diced
2 **red chiles**, seeded and finely chopped
4 cups **vegetable stock**
3 cups **tomato juice** or **tomato puree**
2 tablespoons **tomato paste**
2 tablespoons **sweet chili sauce**
1 (14 oz) can **red kidney beans**, drained
2 tablespoons finely chopped fresh **cilantro**
sea salt and **black pepper**

To serve
⅓ cup **sour cream**
tortilla chips
finely grated **lime** zest

Heat the oil in a large saucepan over medium heat and add the onion. Cook for 5 minutes, stirring frequently, until softened. Add the garlic, bell peppers, and chiles and cook for another 3–4 minutes.

Stir in the stock, tomato juice or puree, tomato paste, chili sauce, kidney beans, and cilantro and bring to a boil. Reduce the heat, cover, and simmer for 20 minutes. Let cool slightly.

Place the soup in a blender or food processor, in batches if necessary, and blend until smooth. Return the soup to the pan and reheat. Season to taste and add a little extra chili sauce, if necessary.

Ladle the soup into warm bowls and swirl a little sour cream into each portion. Serve with tortilla chips and a sprinkling of finely grated lime zest.

HEARTY KALE SOUP WITH GARLIC CROUTONS

This delicious soup is rich in nutrients and flavor but low in calories. It's perfect for stressful, busy days.

Preparation time: 20–25 minutes
Cooking time: 50 minutes
Serves 4
....

4 tablespoons **butter**
1 **onion**, chopped
2 unpeeled **carrots**, sliced
10 oz **kale**, thick stems discarded
2½ cups **water**
1¾ cups **vegetable stock**
finely grated zest and juice of 1 **lemon**
1 **potato**, sliced
pinch of **grated nutmeg**
sea salt and **black pepper**

To serve
3-4 slices of **whole-wheat bread**, crusts removed
3-4 tablespoons **olive oil**
2 **garlic cloves**, sliced
2 **kale leaves**, thinly shredded

Melt the butter in a large saucepan over medium heat and add the onion. Cook for 5 minutes, stirring frequently, until softened. Add the carrots and kale and cook for 2 minutes, stirring constantly.
....

Add the measured water, stock, lemon zest, lemon juice, potatoes, and nutmeg and season to taste. Bring to a boil, stirring from time to time. Reduce the heat, cover, and simmer for 35 minutes or until the vegetables are tender. Let cool slightly.
....

To make the croutons, cut the bread into ½ inch cubes. Heat the oil in a large skillet over medium heat, add the garlic, and cook for 1 minute. Add the bread squares and cook, turning frequently, until evenly browned. Remove from the pan and drain on paper towels. Discard the garlic.
....

Add the shredded kale to the skillet and cook, stirring constantly, until crispy. Drain on paper towels.
....

Place the soup in a blender or food processor, in batches if necessary, and blend until smooth, adding a little extra water if it is too thick. Reheat the soup without boiling. Serve in warm bowls with the garlic croutons and crispy kale.
....

CREAMY KALE, WHITE BEAN & ROSEMARY SOUP

This is a warming, satisfying soup any time of year, full of fiber and stimulating rosemary.

Preparation time: 10 minutes
Cooking time: 25–30 minutes
Serves 4

⋯⋯⋯⋯⋯

2 tablespoons **olive oil**
1 large **onion**, sliced
3 **garlic cloves**, finely chopped
2 (15 oz) cans **cannellini beans**,
  rinsed and drained
2 **bay leaves**
1 tablespoon **dried rosemary**
1 teaspoon **dried thyme**
4 cups **vegetable stock**
3 cups coarsely chopped **kale**
sea salt and **black pepper**
crusty whole-wheat bread, to serve

Heat the olive oil in a large saucepan over medium heat and add the onion. Cook for 5 minutes, stirring frequently, until softened. Add the garlic and cook for another 2 minutes.

⋯⋯⋯⋯⋯⋯⋯⋯⋯⋯⋯⋯⋯⋯

Add two-thirds of the beans to the pan with the bay leaves, rosemary, thyme, and stock. Bring to a boil, reduce the heat, and simmer for 15 minutes. Let cool slightly.

⋯⋯⋯⋯⋯⋯⋯⋯⋯⋯⋯⋯⋯⋯⋯⋯

Place the soup in a blender or food processor, in batches if necessary, and blend until smooth. Return to the pan, season to taste, and add the reserved beans and the kale. Cook for 4–5 minutes, until the kale has wilted. Serve immediately with crusty whole-wheat bread.

⋯⋯⋯⋯⋯⋯⋯⋯⋯⋯⋯⋯⋯⋯⋯⋯

ITALIAN TOMATO & BEAN SOUP

A hearty, filling soup rich in chromium, which balances blood sugar levels and keeps cravings at bay.

Preparation time: 10 minutes
Cooking time: 25–30 minutes
Serves 4
....

1 tablespoon **olive oil**
1 large **onion**, chopped
4 **garlic cloves**, coarsely chopped
2 **celery sticks**, coarsely chopped
1 unpeeled **carrot**, diced
1 (14½ oz) can **diced tomatoes**
8 slow-roasted **tomatoes** or **sun-dried tomatoes** (not in oil), chopped
2 cups canned **mixed beans**, such as pinto beans, black-eyed peas, kidney beans, or chickpeas, rinsed and drained
1 tablespoon chopped **oregano**
3 cups **vegetable stock**
sea salt and **black pepper**

To serve
¼ cup **ricotta cheese**
store-bought **pesto** or **basil oil**
crusty **bread**

Heat the oil in a large saucepan over medium heat and add the onion, garlic, celery, and carrots. Loosely cover and cook for 7–8 minutes, stirring occasionally, until softened and lightly browned.
....

Add all the tomatoes, beans, oregano, and stock and bring to a boil. Reduce the heat and simmer gently for 15–20 minutes, or until the vegetables are tender.
....

Put the soup into a blender or food processor, in batches if necessary, and blend until smooth. Season to taste and ladle into warm soup bowls. Top each bowl with a spoonful of ricotta and a drizzle of pesto or basil oil. Serve with crusty bread.
....

BEEF & BARLEY BROTH

Barley is a potent source of the B vitamins and fiber and adds a wonderful texture to this rich, tasty meal in a bowl.

Preparation time: 10 minutes
Cooking time: 2 hours
Serves 4

2 tablespoons **butter**
8 oz **boneless beef chuck**, diced
1 large **onion**, finely chopped
½ **rutabaga**, peeled and diced
4 unpeeled **carrots**, diced
½ cup **pearl barley**
8 cups **beef stock**
2 teaspoons **dry mustard** (optional)
sea salt and **black pepper**
chopped **parsley**, to garnish

Heat the butter in a large saucepan over medium-high heat, add the beef and onion, and cook for 5 minutes, stirring frequently, until the beef is browned and the onion just beginning to color.

Stir in the diced vegetables, pearl barley, stock, and mustard, if using. Season to taste and bring to a boil. Reduce the heat, cover, and simmer for 1¾ hours, stirring occasionally, until the meat and vegetables are tender.

Ladle the soup into warm bowls and garnish with a little chopped parsley.

BUTTERFLIED SARDINES WITH BEET SALSA

A winning combination of omega-rich sardines and high-fiber beet. Ask a fish dealer to prepare the sardines for you.

Preparation time: 15 minutes
Cooking time: 2-3 minutes
Serves 4

2 tablespoons finely chopped **parsley**
finely grated zest of 1 **lemon**
2 teaspoons **lemon juice**
1 teaspoon **harissa paste**
2 **garlic cloves**, finely chopped
1 tablespoon **extra virgin canola oil**
8-12 **sardines**, scaled and butterflied
2 tablespoons chopped **dill**
sea salt and **black pepper**
ciabatta, toasted, to serve

Beet salsa
2½ cups diced **cooked beets**
   (not in vinegar)
½ **red onion**, minced
1 tablespoon **mature sherry vinegar**
2 tablespoons **baby capers**,
   rinsed and drained

Put the parsley into a bowl with the lemon zest and juice, the harissa, garlic, and oil. Season to taste and stir well. Add the sardines, mix to coat, and set aside.

Put all the salsa ingredients into a bowl, season to taste, and toss to combine.

Arrange the sardines on an aluminum foil-lined broiler pan and place under a preheated hot broiler for 2-3 minutes, turning once, until just cooked through.

Place the sardines on serving plates with the beet salsa and sprinkle with the dill. Serve with toasted ciabatta.

ROASTED PEPPERS WITH TAPENADE

Bell peppers are rich in antioxidants to boost energy levels, overall health, and immunity. Here, they are roasted and combined with energy-lifting olives.

Preparation time: 15 minutes
Cooking time: 45 minutes
Serves 4
....

4 **red bell peppers**, halved lengthwise, cored and seeded
3 tablespoons **olive oil**
1 cup pitted **black ripe olives**
2 **garlic cloves**, coarsely chopped
1 tablespoon chopped **oregano**
¼ cup **tomato paste**
8 oz **tofu**
12 **cherry tomatoes**, halved
sea salt and **black pepper**
chopped **parsley**, to serve

Put the bell peppers, cut side up, in a roasting pan, drizzle with 1 tablespoon of the oil, and season to taste. Place in a preheated oven, at 400°F, for 25–30 minutes, until lightly browned.
....

To make the tapenade, put the olives, garlic, oregano, tomato paste, and remaining olive oil in a blender or food processor and blend to a thick paste, scraping down the mixture from the sides of the bowl.
....

Pat the tofu dry on paper towels and cut into ½ inch dice. Toss in a bowl with the tapenade. Pile the mixture into the bell peppers with the cherry tomatoes and return to the oven for another 15 minutes, until the tomatoes have softened and the filling is hot. Serve sprinkleed generously with parsley.
....

SMOKED CHICKEN WITH BEANS, WALNUTS & TARRAGON

A deliciously fragrant meal to encourage sleep, ease anxiety, support the liver, and balance blood sugar and hormones.

Preparation time: 15 minutes
Cooking time: 3-4 minutes
Serves 4
....

2 cups fine **green beans**, trimmed
1 ripe **avocado**, peeled and pitted
1 tablespoon **lemon juice**
6 cups **mixed salad greens**
2 cups coarsely chopped **hot-smoked chicken breast**
1 **yellow bell pepper**, cored, seeded, and finely chopped
½ cup **walnut pieces**
1 **shallot**, finely chopped
2 teaspoons chopped **tarragon**
4 teaspoons **walnut oil**
sea salt and **black pepper**

To serve
lemon wedges
whole-grain bread

Cook the green beans in a saucepan of lightly salted boiling water for 3-4 minutes, until just tender. Drain and refresh under cold running water.
....

Meanwhile, dice the avocado and toss in the lemon juice to prevent it from discoloring. Put into a large bowl with the salad greens, chicken, bell pepper, walnuts, and beans and toss gently until well combined.
....

Divide among 4 serving plates and sprinkle with the shallot and tarragon. Season to taste and drizzle with the walnut oil. Serve immediately with lemon wedges and whole-grain bread.
....

WATERMELON, POMEGRANATE & CHEESE SALAD

Light and fruity, this wonderful salad blends sweet and savory flavors and a host of immune- and energy-boosting nutrients.

Preparation time: 15 minutes
Cooking time: 4 minutes
Serves 4
....

8 oz **haloumi, mozzarella, or Muenster cheese**, cut into 8 slices
finely grated zest and juice of 1 **lime**
2 **scallions**, finely sliced
2 tablespoons chopped **parsley**
2 tablespoons chopped **mint**
1 tablespoon **avocado oil**
5 cups **arugula**
½ **watermelon**, peeled, seeded, and diced
½ small **red onion**, finely sliced
1 cup **almond-stuffed green olives**
1 tablespoon **pomegranate molasses**
1–2 teaspoons **chili paste**
seeds from 1 **pomegranate**
sea salt and **black pepper**

Place the cheese in a bowl with the lime zest, scallions, and half the herbs and drizzle with a little of the avocado oil. Toss gently to coat, then arrange on an aluminum foil-lined broiler pan. Place under a preheated hot broiler for 3–4 minutes, turning once, until lightly toasted.

Meanwhile, arrange the arugula leaves on 4 large plates. Put the watermelon, onion, olives, and remaining parsley and mint into a large bowl, mix to combine, and spoon the mixture over the arugula.

Put the lime juice, pomegranate molasses, remaining avocado oil, and the chili paste into a small bowl, mix well, and season to taste.

Arrange the broiled cheese on top of the salads and sprinkle with the pomegranate seeds. Drizzle with the dressing and serve immediately.

ROASTED VEGETABLE, FETA & BARLEY SALAD

This antioxidant-rich salad can be eaten warm or cold, as an accompaniment or as a main dish in its own right.

Preparation time: 20 minutes
Cooking time: 40 minutes
Serves 4

1 **red bell pepper**, cored, seeded, and cut into chunks
1 **yellow bell pepper**, cored, seeded, and cut into chunks
1 large **red onion**, cut into chunks
1 large **zucchini**, cut into chunks
1 small **eggplant**, cut into chunks
3 **large garlic cloves**, chopped
¾ cup **olive oil**
2 teaspoons **sea salt**
2 teaspoons **black pepper**
1 cup **pearl barley**
finely grated zest and juice of 1 **lemon**
large bunch of **chives**, finely chopped
1 **red chile**, seeded and finely chopped
⅔ cup **pine nuts**, toasted
10 oz **feta cheese**, cut into chunks
small bunch of **basil**, chopped

Put the bell peppers, onion, zucchini, eggplant, and garlic in a roasting pan and drizzle with half the olive oil, half the salt, and half the black pepper. Toss with your hands to coat. Place in a preheated oven, at 425°F, for 30–40 minutes, stirring occasionally, until the vegetables are beginning to brown at the edges.

Cook the barley in a saucepan of lightly salted boiling water according to package directions. Drain, rinse, and put into a large salad bowl.

Put the remaining olive oil, salt and black pepper, lemon zest, lemon juice, chives, and chile in a bowl, stir together, and set aside.

Put the vegetables and any juices into the bowl with the barley and stir to combine. Pour the dressing over the barley and stir again. Add the pine nuts, feta cheese, and basil and toss gently before serving.

BEET & ORANGE SALAD

The vivid colors of this fresh salad highlight its high antioxidant content, which boosts immunity and supports health on all levels.

Preparation time: 15 minutes
Cooking time: 30 minutes
Serves 4
....

12 small **beets**
2 teaspoons **cumin seeds**
2 tablespoons **red wine vinegar**
3½ cups **watercress**
3 **oranges**, peeled and segmented
4 oz **soft goat cheese**
sea salt and **black pepper**

Dressing
1 tablespoon **honey**
1 teaspoon **whole-grain mustard**
1½ tablespoons **white wine vinegar**
3 tablespoons **olive oil**

Scrub the beets and put into an aluminum foil-lined roasting pan with the cumin seeds and vinegar. Place in a preheated oven, at 375°F, for 30 minutes, until tender. Let cool slightly then rub off the skin and cut in half or quarters, depending on their size.
....

Put all the dressing ingredients into a bowl, season to taste, and whisk to combine.
....

Put the watercress into a bowl with the beets and add the dressing. Mix gently to combine. Arrange the oranges on a plate, top with the beet salad, and crumble the cheese over the top. Season with black pepper and serve.
....

TURKEY BURGERS WITH SPICY SALSA

These healthy burgers are served with a chile-rich salsa to boost metabolism and protect against the adverse effects of stress.

Preparation time: 15 minutes
Cooking time: 10 minutes
Serves 4

1 lb **lean ground turkey**
finely grated zest of 1 **lime**
3 **scallions**, finely sliced
1 tablespoon **sweet soy sauce**
   or **ketjap manis**
1 teaspoon **ground cumin**
2 cups fresh **bread crumbs**
1 medium **egg**, lightly beaten
4 **small whole-wheat buns**, halved
   and toasted
2 **Romaine lettuce hearts**, shredded

Salsa
16 **cherry tomatoes**, quartered
1 **red chile**, seeded and finely chopped
2 **scallions**, finely sliced
1 tablespoon **lime juice**
1 tablespoon **sweet soy sauce**
   or **ketjap manis**
small bunch of fresh **cilantro**, chopped
1 ripe **avocado**, peeled, pitted, and diced

Put the ground turkey into a large bowl with the lime zest, scallions, soy sauce, cumin, bread crumbs, and egg. Mix until well combined, then use wet hands to shape into 8 patties.

Transfer the patties to a broiler pan and place under a preheated hot broiler for 3–4 minutes on each side, until golden and cooked through.

Meanwhile, put all the salsa ingredients into a bowl and stir until well combined. Set aside.

Arrange the toasted bun halves, cut side up, on 4 serving plates and top with shredded lettuce. Place a burger on each and top with the salsa. Serve immediately.

BAKED PUMPKIN & GOAT CHEESE

Pumpkin is rich in beta-carotene and antioxidants to boost immunity, ease pain, and regulate blood sugar levels.

Preparation time: 15 minutes
Cooking time: 25–30 minutes
Serves 4
....

5 **beets**, peeled and diced
5 cups peeled and seeded, large
   pumpkin or **butternut squash** dice
1 **red onion**, cut into wedges
2 tablespoons **olive oil**
2 teaspoons **fennel seeds**
2 small **goat cheeses**, 4 oz each
sea salt and **black pepper**
chopped **rosemary**, to garnish

Put the beets, pumpkin, and onion in a large roasting pan, drizzle with the oil, and sprinkle with the fennel seeds. Season to taste and place in a preheated oven, at 400°F, for 20–25 minutes, turning once, until golden and tender.

....

Cut the goat cheeses in half and nestle the pieces among the roasted vegetables. Season the cheeses and spoon some of the pan juices over them.

....

Return the pan to the oven for about 5 minutes, until the cheese is just beginning to melt. Sprinkle with rosemary and serve immediately.

....

BAKED BARLEY RISOTTO WITH LEEKS, PEAS & SQUASH

Bursting with fiber, the B vitamins, and antioxidants, this risotto will leave you satisfied and ready for a great night's sleep.

Preparation time: 10 minutes
Cooking time: 35–40 minutes
Serves 4

4 oz **unsmoked bacon**, chopped
1 large **leek**, trimmed,
    cleaned and finely sliced
1 tablespoon **dried thyme**
1¼ cups **pearl barley**
2 cups hot **chicken stock**
1 **small butternut squash**, peeled,
    seeded, and cut into chunks
⅔ cup **frozen peas**
½ cup **Parmesan cheese**
sea salt and **black pepper**
2 tablespoons chopped **thyme**, to garnish

Heat a large, heavy saucepan over medium heat, add the bacon, and cook until crispy. Add the leeks and thyme and cook for 3–5 minutes, until beginning to soften.

Stir in the barley, toss to coat in the oil, then add the hot chicken stock. Bring to a boil, then stir in the butternut squash. Transfer the mixture to a large ovenproof dish and cover with aluminum foil. Place in a preheated oven, at 425°F, for 15 minutes.

Remove the foil and stir in the peas. Cover again and return to the oven for another 10–15 minutes, until the stock has been absorbed and the barley is tender. Stir in the Parmesan, season to taste, and serve immediately, sprinkled with thyme.

CHICKPEA, ALMOND & PARMESAN PASTA

This is an inventive combination of high-calcium almonds and digestion- and energy-boosting chickpeas in a quick pasta dish.

Preparation time: 10 minutes
Cooking time: 15 minutes
Serves 4
....

1 tablespoon **olive oil**
3 **garlic cloves**, finely chopped
6 cups **vegetable stock**
1 large **red chile**, seeded
    and finely chopped
1 lb **whole-wheat spaghetti** or **linguine**
1 (15 oz) can **chickpeas**, rinsed and drained
½ cup finely grated **Parmesan cheese**
sea salt and **black pepper**
¾ cup chopped **almonds**, toasted, to serve

Heat the olive oil in a large saucepan over medium heat, add the garlic, and cook for 1–2 minutes, until softened. Add the stock and chile and bring to a boil.
....

Add the pasta and cook, uncovered, according to package directions until al dente. By this time most of the stock will have been absorbed.
....

Add the chickpeas and warm through. Season to taste, then stir in the Parmesan. Serve immediately, sprinkled with the almonds.
....

BUTTERNUT SQUASH STEW WITH HERB QUINOA

This vegetarian feast is high in protein, antioxidants, cleansing herbs, and warming spices to balance blood sugar.

Preparation time: 15 minutes
Cooking time: 45 minutes–1 hour
Serves 4

2 tablespoons **olive oil**
2 large **onions**, thinly sliced
2 teaspoons **ground cumin**
2 teaspoons **ground coriander**
2 teaspoons **ground cinnamon**
3 **garlic cloves**, sliced
3 tablespoons **harissa paste**
1 large **butternut squash**, peeled, seeded, and cut into chunks
4 unpeeled **carrots**, cut into chunks
2 **celery sticks**, sliced
½ cup **dried apricots**
2½ cups **vegetable stock**
1 (15 oz) can **chickpeas**, rinsed and drained
¼ cup chopped **flat leaf parsley**
sea salt and **black pepper**
⅔ cup chopped **fresh cilantro**, to serve

Quinoa
1½ cups **quinoa**
1 **vegetable bouillon cube**
¼ cup **parsley**, chopped
½ cup **mint**, chopped
⅓ cup **fresh cilantro**, chopped
⅓ cup **pine nuts**, toasted
seeds from 1 large **pomegranate**

Heat the olive oil in a large saucepan over medium heat, add the onions, and cook for 5–10 minutes, until soft. Add the spices and garlic and continue cooking for another 3–4 minutes, until fragrant.

Stir in the harissa paste and cook for 3 minutes, stirring constantly, then add the squash, carrots, and celery, and cook for another 5 minutes, stirring frequently.

Add the apricots and stock and bring to a boil. Reduce the heat, cover the pan, and simmer for 20 minutes. Add the chickpeas, cover again, and cook for another 10 minutes or until the vegetables are tender.

Meanwhile, cook the quinoa in a saucepan of lightly salted boiling water according to package directions, crumbling the bouillon cube into the cooking water. Drain but do not rinse the cooked quinoa, then stir in the herbs and pine nuts. Set aside and keep warm.

Add the parsley to the stew, season to taste, and sprinkle with the fresh cilantro. Serve with the quinoa, sprinkled with the pomegranate seeds.

HALIBUT WITH MUSTARD & CURRY LEAVES

A fragrant curry containing four superfoods—halibut, onions, chiles, and coconut—recommended for fighting fatigue.

Preparation time: 20 minutes
Cooking time: 25–30 minutes
Serves 4

1 teaspoon **ground turmeric**
1 tablespoon **chili powder**
2 tablespoons grated **fresh coconut**
¼ cup **vegetable oil**
1 teaspoon **black mustard seeds**
20 **fresh curry leaves**
2 **onions**, thinly sliced
4 **green chiles**, seeded and sliced
1 inch piece of **fresh ginger root**,
    peeled and cut into matchsticks
6 **garlic cloves**, finely chopped
2 lb **skinless halibut fillet**,
    cut into bite-size pieces
1¾ cups **coconut milk**
1¼ cups **water**
1 tablespoon **tamarind paste**
sea salt
steamed **basmati rice** or **long-grain rice**,
    to serve

Mix the turmeric, chili powder, and grated coconut in a small bowl and set aside.

Heat the oil in a large wok or heavy saucepan over medium-high heat, add the mustard seeds, and cook for a few minutes, until the seeds begin to pop. Add the curry leaves, onions, green chiles, ginger, and garlic and stir-fry for about 5 minutes, until fragrant.

Stir in the turmeric mixture and cook, stirring continually, for another 1 minute. Add the fish, then stir in the coconut milk and measured water. Finally, add the tamarind paste and bring to a boil.

Reduce the heat and simmer gently for 15 minutes or until the fish is cooked through. Season to taste and ladle into warmebowls. Serve with steamed basmati or long-grain rice.

SPICED HALIBUT & OYSTERS WITH BEET SALAD

Packed full of nutrients to lift energy levels, this spicy halibut dish will support everything from the adrenal glands to the liver.

Preparation time: 25 minutes, plus marinating
Cooking time: 1¼ hours
Serves 6
....

½ teaspoon **ground cumin**
½ teaspoon **ground coriander**
½ teaspoon **paprika**
½ teaspoon **cayenne pepper**
½ teaspoon **sea salt**
½ teaspoon **garam masala**
1 tablespoon **whole-wheat flour**
4 **skinless halibut fillets,** about 5 oz each
12–16 **oysters**, shucked
2 tablespoons **olive oil**
sea salt and **black pepper**

Salad
1¼ lb **beets**
1 tablespoon chopped **thyme**
6 **garlic cloves**, chopped
⅓ cup **olive oil**
1 tablespoon **cumin seeds**, toasted
finely grated zest and juice of 1 **lemon**
½ cup **Greek yogurt with live active cultures**
2 tablespoons chopped **fresh cilantro**

Put the spices, salt, garam masala, and flour into a large bowl and mix well. Pat the halibut and oysters dry with paper towels and toss in the seasoned flour, rubbing it into the flesh. Cover and put into the refrigerator for 1 hour to marinate.
....

Put the whole, unpeeled beets in a roasting pan and sprinkle with the thyme and garlic. Drizzle over half the olive oil and cover with aluminum foil. Place in a preheated oven, at 350°F, for 1 hour until tender. Let cool a little, then peel and cut into chunks. Place the cumin seeds, remaining olive oil, lemon juice, and lemon zest in a small bowl and season to taste. Pour the dressing over the beet and toss well. Put the yogurt into a bowl with the cilantro, season to taste, and stir into the beets.
....

Heat the olive oil in a large skillet over high heat and add the halibut. Cook for about 6 minutes, until golden underneath, then carefully turn over.
....

Reduce the heat to medium, add the oysters, and cook for another 4 minutes, until the fish flakes easily when tested with a fork and the oysters are just cooked through. Serve with the beet salad.
....

FLOUNDER WITH VEGETABLES PROVENÇAL

All types of fish encourage good energy levels and reduce the symptoms that can underpin low mood and fatigue.

Preparation time: 15 minutes
Cooking time: 45–50 minutes
Serves 4
....

2 **zucchini**, sliced
1 **eggplant**, sliced
4 **tomatoes**, quartered
1 **onion**, thickly sliced
1 large **red bell pepper**, cored, seeded, and sliced
3 **garlic cloves**, sliced
small bunch of **basil**, chopped, plus extra, shredded, to garnish
1 tablespoon chopped **thyme**
3 tablespoons chopped **parsley**
3 tablespoons **olive oil**
3 tablespoons **all-purpose flour**
4 **flounder fillets**, about 5 oz each
sea salt and **black pepper**

Put all the vegetables and the chopped herbs into a large roasting pan and season to taste. Drizzle with half the olive oil, toss well to combine, and place in a preheated oven, at 350°F, for 40–45 minutes or until the vegetables are tender.

....

Put the flour on a plate and season to taste. Dust the flounder in the flour, turning to coat all over. Heat the remaining oil in a large, nonstick skillet over medium heat, add the fish, skin side down, and cook for 2–3 minutes.

....

Turn the fish over and cook for another 2–3 minutes, until the flesh flakes easily when tested with a fork.

....

Spoon the vegetables onto 4 serving plates and top with the flounder. Serve immediately, garnished with shredded basil.
....

CREAMY OYSTER STEW WITH KELP RICE

This mouth-watering meal provides a wealth of nutrients, balancing blood sugar and supporting the thyroid.

Preparation time: 20 minutes
Cooking time: 20 minutes
Serves 4

6 tablespoons **butter**
4 **celery sticks**, finely chopped
8 **shallots**, finely chopped
1 **garlic clove**, finely chopped
1 tablespoon **paprika**
⅔ cup **light cream**
1¼ cups **milk**
24 **oysters**, shucked
sea salt and **black pepper**
2 tablespoons chopped **parsley**, to garnish

Rice

1¼ cups **brown rice**
2 tablespoons **olive oil**
1 **small onion**, finely chopped
1 unpeeled **carrot**, finely chopped
3 **garlic cloves**, finely chopped
1 teaspoon **dried thyme**
4 oz **dried kelp**, soaked, drained, and chopped
1 tablespoon **cayenne pepper**

Cook the rice in a large saucepan of lightly salted boiling water until tender, according to package directions.

Heat the oil in a large, heavy saucepan over medium heat, add the onion, carrot, and garlic, and cook for about 7 minutes, until soft. Add the thyme and kelp and cook for another 2 minutes.

Meanwhile, melt the butter in a large saucepan over medium heat, add the celery and shallots, and cook for 5–7 minutes, until soft. Add the garlic and paprika and cook for another 2 minutes.

Add the cream and milk and stir until combined, then bring to a boil. Reduce the heat, add the oysters and their juices, and cook gently until they just begin to curl at the edges. Season to taste.

Drain and rinse the rice and add to the pan with the vegetables and kelp. Season to taste and stir in the cayenne pepper.

Divide the rice among 4 serving plates and top with the oyster stew. Serve immediately, garnished with parsley.

HONEY-GLAZED TUNA WITH PARSNIP PUREE

Tuna is rich in omega-3 oils, encouraging good physical and emotional health and lifting mood and energy levels.

Preparation time: 15 minutes
Cooking time: 25 minutes
Serves 4

1 tablespoon **honey**
2 tablespoons **whole-grain mustard**
1 teaspoon **tomato paste**
2 tablespoons **orange juice**
1 tablespoon **red wine vinegar**
    or balsamic vinegar
4 **tuna steaks**, about 5 oz each
2 teaspoons **olive oil**
sea salt and **black pepper**
steamed **green vegetables**, to serve

Parsnip puree
2 unpeeled **parsnips**, cut into chunks
2 **potatoes**, cut into chunks
¼ cup **plain yogurt with live active cultures**
2 teaspoons **horseradish sauce** (optional)

Put the honey, mustard, tomato paste, orange juice, and vinegar into a small saucepan over medium heat and bring to a boil. Reduce the heat and simmer until the mixture reduces to a syrupy glaze. Keep warm.

To make the parsnip puree, cook the parsnips and potatoes in a steamer set over a saucepan of gently simmering water until tender. Drain and put into a blender or food processor with the yogurt and horseradish sauce, if using. Season to taste and blend until just smooth. Keep warm.

Brush the tuna with the olive oil and season to taste. Cook in a preheated hot ridged grill pan or under a preheated hot broiler for 1-2 minutes, until lightly charred. Turn and spoon a little of the glaze over the tuna. Cook for another 1-2 minutes, until golden on the outside but still pink in the center.

To serve, divide the parsnip puree among 4 warmed serving plates, top with the tuna steaks, and drizzle with the remaining glaze. Serve with steamed green vegetables.

SALMON WITH HORSERADISH CRUST

Salmon is a functional food with many benefits, from pain relief and weight control to enhanced immunity, energy levels, and adrenal function.

Preparation time: 10 minutes
Cooking time: 15 minutes
Serves 4

....

4 **salmon fillets**, about 7 oz each
¼ cup **mild horseradish sauce**
2¾ cups **fresh bread crumbs**
20 **asparagus spears**, trimmed
1 tablespoon **olive oil**
¼–⅓ cup **crème fraîche**
¼ cup **lemon juice**
1 tablespoon chopped **parsley**,
  plus few sprigs to garnish
sea salt and **black pepper**

Put the salmon fillets in an ovenproof dish, skin side down. Spread the top of each fillet with 1 tablespoon of the horseradish sauce, then sprinkle with the bread crumbs. Place in a preheated oven, at 350°F, for 12–15 minutes, until the fish is just cooked and the bread crumbs are golden.

....

Meanwhile, blanch the asparagus in a large saucepan of lightly salted boiling water for 2 minutes. Drain well and place in a preheated hot ridged grill pan with the oil until lightly charred, turning regularly. Season to taste.

....

Put the crème fraîche, lemon juice, and chopped parsley into a small bowl, season to taste, and stir to combine. Garnish with the parsley sprigs and serve alongside the salmon and the chargrilled asparagus.

....

HERBED CHICKEN & RICOTTA CANNELLONI

A comforting, cheesy pasta dish made with whole-wheat cannelloni, which will help keep your blood sugar levels constant.

Preparation time: 20 minutes
Cooking time: 45–55 minutes
Serves 4
....

2 tablespoons **olive oil**
1 lb **boneless, skinless chicken thighs**,
    finely chopped or ground
2 **leeks**, trimmed, cleaned and diced
2 cups **tomato puree** or **tomato sauce**
⅓ cup chopped **mixed herbs**,
    such as parsley, chives,
    sage, marjoram, and dill
1 teaspoon **fennel seeds**
8 oz **ricotta cheese**
finely grated zest of 1 **lemon**
½ teaspoon **grated nutmeg**
1 teaspoon **paprika**
3½ cups **frozen spinach**, defrosted
1½ cups **sun-dried tomatoes**
    (not in oil), chopped
8 oz **whole-wheat cannelloni**
2–3 tablespoons finely grated
    Parmesan cheese
sea salt and **black pepper**
green salad, to serve

Heat half the oil in a large, nonstick skillet over medium-high heat, add the chicken, and cook for 3–4 minutes or until browned, stirring frequently. Reduce the heat, add the leeks, and cook for another 3–4 minutes.

Meanwhile, heat the tomato puree or sauce in a saucepan over medium heat and stir in one-third of the chopped herbs, the fennel seeds, and the remaining oil. Bring to a boil, season to taste, then reduce the heat and simmer gently for 2–3 minutes.

Remove the chicken from the heat and stir in the ricotta, the remaining chopped herbs, the lemon zest, nutmeg, paprika, spinach, and sun-dried tomatoes. Season to taste. Stand the cannelloni tubes upright and use a spoon to fill them with the ricotta mixture.

Spoon half the tomato puree over the bottom of a shallow ovenproof dish. Arrange the filled pasta tubes, side by side, in the dish in one closely fitting layer. Pour the remaining tomato puree over the top of the cannelloni, then sprinkle with the Parmesan.

Place in a preheated oven, at 350°F, for 35–40 minutes, until bubbling. Serve hot with a crisp green salad.

CHORIZO, CHICKPEA & RED PEPPER STEW

Fiber, antioxidants, and knockout Mediterranean flavors make this a great choice for a healthy energy-boosting supper.

Preparation time: 10 minutes
Cooking time: 25 minutes
Serves 4

....

1 lb **new potatoes**
1 teaspoon **olive oil**
2 **red onions**, chopped
2 **red bell peppers**, cored,
   seeded, and chopped
4 oz **chorizo**, thinly sliced
8 **plum tomatoes**, chopped,
   or 1 (14½ oz) can **diced tomatoes**
1 (15 oz) can **chickpeas**,
   rinsed and drained
sea salt and **black pepper**
2 tablespoons chopped **parsley,** to garnish
crusty bread, to serve

Cook the potatoes in a saucepan of lightly salted boiling water for 12–15 minutes, until tender. Drain, then slice.

....

Meanwhile, heat the oil in a large skillet, add the onions and bell peppers, and cook for 3–4 minutes, until beginning to soften. Add the chorizo and continue to cook for 2 minutes.

....

Add the potato slices, tomatoes, and chickpeas, bring to a boil, and simmer for 10 minutes. Season to taste, sprinkle with the parsley, and serve with bread.

....

BRAISED TURKEY WITH YOGURT & POMEGRANATE

Tryptophan-rich turkey and soothing yogurt encourage restful sleep, while pomegranate provides a burst of antioxidants.

Preparation time: 15 minutes
Cooking time: 45 minutes
Serves 4

12 oz **boneless, skinless turkey breast and thigh**, cut into large chunks
1 teaspoon **ground cumin**
1 teaspoon **ground coriander**
1 teaspoon **ground cinnamon**
1 tablespoon **olive oil**
1 large **onion**, sliced
1 **red chile**, seeded and finely chopped
8 **garlic cloves**, finely chopped
1¾ cups **chicken stock**
1 **rosemary sprig**
1 tablespoon **cornstarch**
1 cup **Greek yogurt with live active cultures**
seeds from 1 large **pomegranate**
sea salt and **black pepper**
chopped **fresh cilantro**, to garnish

Put the turkey into a bowl with the cumin, ground coriander, and cinnamon, season to taste, and toss to coat.

Heat the oil in a large saucepan over high heat, add the turkey ,and cook, stirring constantly, until golden. Remove from the pan and set aside.

Reduce the heat to medium-low, add the onion to the pan, and cook for 5–10 minutes, until soft. Add the chile and garlic and cook for another 2–3 minutes. Return the turkey and any juices to the pan, add the stock and rosemary, and bring to a boil. Reduce the heat and simmer, uncovered, for 15 minutes, stirring frequently, until the turkey is cooked through.

Remove the turkey from the pan with a slotted spoon and keep warm. Increase the heat, bring the liquid to a boil, and cook until reduced by about half.

Place the cornstarch and yogurt in a bowl and stir to combine. Add to the pan, reduce the heat to low, and stir until the sauce has thickened. Return the turkey to the pan and stir well. Transfer to a serving dish and sprinkle with the pomegranate seeds. Garnish with fresh cilantro.

THAI FRUIT SKEWERS

Rich in nutrients to improve overall health and boost digestion, these fruit skewers also contain immune-boosting vitamin C.

Preparation time: 15 minutes
Cooking time: 1–2 minutes
Serves 4
....

4 long **lemon grass stalks**
2 **kiwifruit**, peeled and cut into chunks
2 **mangos**, peeled, pitted,
   and cut into chunks
1 **papaya**, peeled, seeded,
   and cut into chunks
½ **pineapple**, peeled, cored,
   and cut into chunks
2 tablespoons packed **light brown sugar**
2 tablespoons **dried coconut**
vanilla yogurt, to serve

Cut the lemon grass stalks into 8 inch lengths and cut each in half lengthwise. Remove the tough outer layers and trim the thin ends to a point.

....

Thread the fruit onto the 8 skewers, then arrange in a single layer on a baking sheet. Put the sugar and coconut into a small bowl, stir to mix, then sprinkle over the fruit.

....

Place under a preheated hot broiler for 1–2 minutes or until the sugar is caramelized and the coconut is toasted. Serve immediately with vanilla yogurt.

....

CHOCOLATE CHILE DESSERTS

These fiery, sweet little desserts are rich in mood-lifting, energy-boosting nutrients to satisfy cravings and help ease chronic pain.

Preparation time: 10 minutes, plus chilling
Cooking time: 10 minutes
Serves 4
....

1 large **dried red chile**
1¼ cups **light cream**
8 oz **semisweet dark chocolate**,
    broken into pieces
3 **egg yolks**, lightly beaten
3 tablespoons **sugar**
2 tablespoons **butter**, softened
1 small **fresh red chile**, minced, to garnish

Put the dried chile and cream in a small saucepan over medium heat and bring to a boil. Remove from the heat and discard the chile. Stir in the chocolate until melted and smooth.
....

Put the egg yolks, sugar, and butter into a small bowl and whisk until light and fluffy. Fold into the melted chocolate mixture and pour into 4 ramekins or small serving bowls.
....

Chill in the refrigerator for 1 hour, then top each portion with a sprinkling of fresh chile. Chill for another 2 hours, or until set.
....

FRUITY FROZEN YOGURT

This dessert takes only minutes to make and will help enhance energy levels, boost immunity, and balance blood sugar.

Preparation time: 10 minutes, plus freezing
Serves 4

4 cups **frozen berries**, such as strawberries, blueberries, raspberries, and blackberries
¼ cup **confectioners' sugar**
1 cup **plain yogurt with live active cultures**
finely grated zest and juice of ½ **lemon**

Put all the ingredients into a blender or food processor and blend until smooth.

Transfer to a shallow, freezerproof container. Freeze for about 40 minutes, until firm, stirring once. Serve immediately, or store in the freezer and defrost for 20 minutes to soften before serving.

STRAWBERRY & RASPBERRY ROULADE

Antioxidant- and fiber-rich berries combined with digestion-soothing yogurt make this roulade a healthy, energizing treat.

Preparation time: 30 minutes, plus cooling
Cooking time: 8 minutes
Makes 16 slices

....

oil or **butter**, for greasing
3 **eggs**
⅔ cup **superfine** or **granulated sugar**
1 cup **whole-wheat flour**
1 tablespoon hot **water**
2 cups quartered **strawberries**,
    defrosted if frozen
2 cups **raspberries**, defrosted if frozen
1 cup **plain yogurt with live active cultures**
confectioners' sugar, for dusting

Grease a 13 x 9 inch jellyroll pan. Line with nonstick parchment paper to come about ½ inch above the sides of the pan, then lightly grease the paper.

....

Put the eggs and sugar into a bowl set over a saucepan of hot water and beat, using a handheld electric mixer, until pale and thick. Sift the flour and fold into the egg mixture with the measured hot water.

....

Pour the batter into the pan and place in a preheated oven, at 425°F, for 8 minutes, until golden and set.

Meanwhile, cut a sheet of nonstick parchment paper 1 inch larger all around than the jellyroll pan. Place it on top of a clean damp dish towel. As soon as it comes out of the oven, turn out the sponge face down onto this sheet of parchment paper, and peel the lining paper off the back of the sponge. Roll the sponge up tightly with the new paper inside. Wrap the dish towel around the outside and place on a wire rack to cool.

....

Place half the berries in a bowl with the yogurt and mix well. Unroll the sponge, then spread with the berry mixture. Roll the sponge up again, trim the ends, and transfer to a serving plate. Dust with confectioners' sugar.

....

Place the remaining berries in a blender or food processor and blend until smooth. Serve as a sauce with the roulade.

....

APRICOT & COCONUT PUDDING

This fatigue-busting pudding is light enough to enjoy after even the heaviest meal and will give the liver and thyroid gland a boost.

Preparation time: 15 minutes,
  plus cooling and chilling
Cooking time: 15 minutes
Serves 4
....

1 cup **unsweetened soy milk**
1¾ cups **coconut milk**
1½ cups chopped **dried apricots**
2 **fresh apricots**, peeled,
  pitted, and chopped
2 tablespoons **maple syrup**
finely grated zest and juice of ½ **lemon**
1 tablespoon **vanilla extract**
2 tablespoons **cornstarch**
¼ teaspoon **sea salt**
¼ cup **water**

Put the soy and coconut milks into a saucepan over medium heat and bring to a boil. Stir in the dried apricots, reduce the heat, and simmer for 5 minutes. Let cool to room temperature, then chill in the refrigerator for 2 hours, until the apricots are moist and plump.

....

Put the milk mixture into a blender or food processor with the fresh apricots, maple syrup, lemon zest, lemon juice, and vanilla and blend until smooth. Return to the saucepan and place over medium heat until simmering, stirring regularly.

....

Put the cornstarch, salt, and measured water into a small bowl and stir until smooth. Slowly pour into the apricot mixture, whisking continuously, until the mixture thickens. Divide among 4 serving bowls, let cool, then chill in the refrigerator for 1 hour, or until ready to serve.

....

PEAR & BLACKBERRY CRISP

A warming crisp dessert with an oaty top that is high in fiber and omega-rich oils to boost concentration and energy levels.

Preparation time: 20 minutes
Cooking time: 30 minutes
Serves 4
....

4 large **pears**, peeled, cored, and finely sliced
2 tablespoons **cornstarch**
2 teaspoons **ground cinnamon**
¼ cup **honey**
1 cup **blackberries**, defrosted if frozen
finely grated zest and juice of 1 **orange**
Greek yogurt with live active cultures, to serve

Topping
2 cups **rolled oats**
2 teaspoons **ground cinnamon**
½ cup **almonds**, crushed
½ cup **walnut pieces**, crushed
2 drops of **vanilla extract**
4 tablespoons **butter**, melted, plus a little extra to dot

Put the pears, cornstarch, cinnamon, and honey into a large bowl and toss together. Add the blackberries, orange zest, and orange juice, toss again, then transfer the mixture to an ovenproof dish.
....

Put all the topping ingredients into a separate bowl, stir to mix, then press the mixture into an even layer on top of the fruit.
....

Dot with a little more butter, then place in a preheated oven, at 400°F, for 30 minutes, until the topping is golden and the fruit juices have started to bubble up around the edges. Serve with yogurt.
....

HOT BLACKBERRY & APPLE TRIFLE

This is comfort food at its finest, packed with antioxidant-rich berries, apples full of fiber, and eggs rich in protein.

Preparation time: 20 minutes
Cooking time: 20–25 minutes
Serves 4
....

1 cup **blackberries**,
   defrosted if frozen
2 **sweet, crisp apples**, cored and sliced
1 tablespoon **water**
¼ cup **sugar**
4 **shortcake sponges or** 16 **ladyfingers**
3 tablespoons **orange juice**
1⅓ cups prepared **custard** or
   vanilla pudding

Meringue
3 **egg whites**
⅓ cup **superfine** or **granulated sugar**

Place the blackberries, apples, measured water, and sugar in a saucepan over medium heat and bring to a boil. Reduce the heat, cover, and simmer for 5 minutes or until the fruit has softened. Let cool slightly.
....

Break the trifle sponges into chunks and arrange in an even layer in the bottom of a 1-quart ovenproof dish. Drizzle the orange juice over the sponges, spoon the poached fruit and juices over the top, then cover with the custard.
....

Whisk the egg whites in a large bowl with a handheld electric mixer until stiff peaks form, then gradually whisk in the sugar, a teaspoonful at a time, until the meringue is stiff and glossy. Spoon over the top of the custard and swirl the top with the back of a spoon.
....

Place in a preheated oven, at 350°F, for 15–20 minutes until heated through and the meringue is golden. Serve immediately.
....

PERFECT PECAN PIES

Pecans are rich in omega oils to boost energy levels and concentration. These healthy little pies are also full of fiber.

Preparation time: 25 minutes,
  plus chilling and cooling
Cooking time: about 20 minutes
Makes 8

½ cup **brown rice flour**,
  plus extra for dusting
½ cup **chickpea (besan) flour**
½ cup **cornmeal**
1 teaspoon **xanthan gum**
1 stick **butter**, cubed
2 tablespoons **superfine** or **granulated sugar**
1 **egg**, beaten
Greek yogurt with live active cultures,
  to serve

Filling
½ cup firmly packed **light brown sugar**
1¼ sticks **butter**
½ cup **honey**
1¾ cups **pecan halves**
2 **eggs**, beaten

Put the flours, polenta, xanthan gum and butter into a blender or food processor and blend until the mixture resembles fine bread crumbs. Alternatively, rub the butter into the dry ingredients by hand.

Stir in the sugar, then add the egg and mix gently using a blunt knife, adding a little cold water, if needed, to form a firm dough.

Dust a work surface with rice flour and knead the dough for 1–2 minutes, then wrap closely in plastic wrap and chill in the refrigerator for 1 hour.

Meanwhile, put the sugar, butter, and honey into a saucepan over low heat and stir until the sugar has dissolved. Let cool for 10 minutes.

Knead the dough again to soften it a little, then divide into 8 equal portions. Roll out each piece on a lightly floured work surface to a thickness of ⅛ inch. Use to line 8 individual pie dishes, about 4½ inches in diameter, rolling the rolling pin over the tops to cut off the excess dough.

Coarsely chop half the pecans. Stir the chopped pecans and eggs into the honey mixture and pour into the pastry-lined dishes. Arrange remaining pecan halves on top.

Place in a preheated oven, at 400°F, for 15–20 minutes, until the filling is firm. Let cool a little, then serve with the Greek yogurt.

ORANGE, RHUBARB & GINGER SLUMP

With fiber-rich rhubarb and oranges, this mood-lifting treat also contains warming ginger to aid digestion, ease pain, and fight candida.

Preparation time: 10 minutes,
Cooking time: 20–25 minutes
Serves 4
....

15 **rhubarb stalks**, cut into ¾ inch pieces
½ inch piece of **fresh ginger root**,
  peeled and finely grated
¼ cup **sugar**
grated zest and juice of 1 **orange**
¼ cup **mascarpone cheese**
1⅓ cups **all-purpose flour**, sifted
1 teaspoon **baking powder**
4 tablespoons **unsalted butter**,
  cut into small pieces
finely grated zest of ½ **lemon**
⅓ cup **milk**
cream, to serve

Put the rhubarb, ginger, half the sugar, the orange zest, and orange juice into a saucepan over medium heat and bring to a boil. Reduce the heat and simmer gently for 5–6 minutes, until the rhubarb is just tender.
....

Transfer the mixture to an ovenproof dish and spoon the mascarpone over it.
....

Put the flour into a bowl with the butter and rub the butter into the flour with the fingertips until the mixture resembles fine bread crumbs. Stir in the remaining sugar, the lemon zest, and milk until combined. Place spoonfuls of the mixture on top of the rhubarb and mascarpone.
....

Place in a preheated oven, at 400°F, for 12–15 minutes, until golden and bubbling. Serve with cream.
....

BEET BROWNIES

These moist brownies are delicious, yet rich in antioxidants, fiber, and nutrients to boost energy levels and mood.

Preparation time: 20 minutes
Cooking time: 30 minutes
Serves 4

2 sticks **butter**, plus extra for greasing
8 oz **semsisweet dark chocolate**
3 tablespoons unsweetened **cocoa powder**
1¼ cups **sugar**
3 **eggs**, lightly beaten
1¼ cups **whole-wheat flour**
1¼ teaspoons **baking powder**
1 teaspoon **ground cinnamon**
1 cup chopped **walnut** pieces
5 **cooked beets** (not in vinegar), peeled and grated

Melt the chocolate and butter in a heat-proof bowl set over a saucepan of lightly simmering water, making sure the water does not touch the bottom of the bowl.

Put the cocoa, sugar, and eggs into a large bowl and beat until light, then stir in the melted chocolate. Sift in the flour, baking powder, and cinnamon, add any bran left in the sifter to the bowl, and stir until combined. Stir in the walnuts and beet.

Spread the mixture into an 8 x 9 inch baking pan lined with nonstick parchment paper and place in a preheated oven, at 350°F, for 20 minutes, until a toothpick inserted into the center comes out almost clean. The brownies should be moist and not fully set. Let cool before cutting into squares.

FIG & WALNUT UPSIDE-DOWN CAKE

This sweet, fragrant cake is utterly delicious, yet bursting with fiber, omega oils, and nutrients to balance blood sugar.

Preparation time: 25 minutes, plus cooling
Cooking time: 45 minutes
Makes 16 slices

....

1 stick **butter**
1 cup firmly packed **light brown sugar**
12 ripe **figs**, stems removed,
   halved lengthwise
3 tablespoons chopped **rosemary**
¼ cup chopped **walnut pieces**
1¼ cups **whole-wheat flour**
1 teaspoon **baking powder**
3 **eggs**, separated
1 cup **sugar**
finely grated zest of 2 **lemons**
¼ cup **lemon juice**
2 teaspoons **vanilla extract**

To serve
plain yogurt with live active cultures
a few drops of **vanilla extract**

Put the butter into a 9 inch round cake pan and place in a preheated oven, at 350°F, for about 5 minutes, until melted. Remove from the oven and press the brown sugar into the bottom of the pan with the back of a spoon. Arrange the figs on top of the sugar, cut side up, and sprinkle with 2 tablespoons of the rosemary and the chopped walnuts. Set aside.

....

Sift the flour and baking powder into a bowl and mix well. Put the egg whites inyo a separate bowl and use a handheld electric mixer to beat until fluffy and beginning to hold their shape. Set aside.

Put the egg yolks and sugar into a large bowl and beat with the handheld electric mixer until fluffy. Stir in the lemon zest, lemon juice, and vanilla with the remaining rosemary. Beat in the flour mixture until well combined, then gently fold in the egg whites. Pour into the cake pan on top of the figs and smooth the surface.

Bake in the oven for 40 minutes, until well risen and golden. Cool in the pan for 10 minutes, then turn out onto a serving plate. Serve warm or cold with yogurt, mixed with a few drops of vanilla extract.

RESOURCES

American Chronic Pain Association
Tel: (800) 533-3231 (toll-free)
E-mail: ACPA@theacpa.org
Web site: www.theacpa.org

American Diabetes Association
Tel: (800) 342-2383 (toll-free)
E-mail: AskADA@diabetes.org
Web site: www.diabetes.org

American Society for Nutrition
Tel: (301) 634-7050
Web site: www.nutrition.org

Anxiety and Depression Association of America
Tel: (240) 485-1001
Web site: www.adaa.org

The Better Sleep Council
Tel: (703) 683-8371
Web site: www.bettersleep.org

Black Women's Health Imperative
Tel: (202) 548-4000
E-mail: info@BlackWomensHealth.org
Web site: www.blackwomenshealth.org

Food and Nutrition Information Center
Tel: (301) 504-5414
E-mail: FNIC@ars.usda.gov
Web site: fnic.nal.usda.gov

Hepatitis Foundation International
Tel: (800) 891-0707 (toll-free)
E-mail: info@hepatitisfoundation.org
Web site: www.hepatitisfoundation.org

International Foundation for Functional Gastrointestinal Disorders
Tel: (888) 964-2001 (toll-free)
Tel: (414) 964-1799 (local)
E-mail: iffgd@iffgd.org
Web site: www.iffgd.org

Mental Health America
Tel: (800) 969-6642 (toll-free)
Tel: (703) 684-7722 (local)
Web site: www.mentalhealthamerica.net

National Alliance for Hispanic Health
Tel: (202) 387-5000
E-mail: alliance@hispanichealth.org
Web site: www.hispanichealth.org

National Alliance on Mental Illness
Tel: (800) 950-6264 (toll-free)
Tel: (703) 524-7600 (local)
Web site: www.nami.org

National Eating Disorders Association
Tel: (800) 931-2237 (toll-free)
Tel: (206) 382-3587 (local)
E-mail: info@NationalEatingDisorders.org
Web site: www.nationaleatingdisorders.org

National Institute of Mental Health
Tel: (866) 615-6464 (toll-free)
Tel: (301) 443-4513 (local)
E-mail: nimhinfo@nih.gov
Web site: www.nimh.nih.gov/index.shtml

National Sleep Foundation
Tel: (703) 243-1697
E-mail: nsf@sleepfoundation.org
Web site: www.sleepfoundation.org

National Women's Health Network
Tel: (202) 682-2640
E-mail: healthquestion@nwhn.org
Web site: nwhn.org

North American Menopause Society
Tel: (800) 774-5342 (toll-free)
Tel: (440) 442-7550 (local)
E-mail: info@menopause.org
Web site: www.menopause.org

North American Vegetarian Society
Tel: (518) 568-7970
Web site: www.navs-online.org

Society for Nutrition Education and Behavior
Tel: (800) 235-6690 (toll-free)
Tel: (317) 328-4627 (local
E-mail: info@sne.org
Web site: www.sne.org

INDEX

Acknowledgments

Gill Paul would like to
thank the very talented
team at Octopus: Denise
Bates, who came up
with the idea for the
series; Katy Denny, Alex
Stetter, and Jo Wilson
who edited the books
so efficiently and made
it all work; and to the
design team of Jonathan
Christie and Isobel de
Cordova for making it all
look so gorgeous. Thank
you also to Karel Bata
for all the support and
for eating my cooking.

Karen Sullivan would
like to thank Cole, Luke,
and Marcus.

Picture credits

Commissioned
photography ©
Octopus Publishing
Group/Will Heap apart
from the following:

Getty Images
Foodcollection 34;
Foodcollection RF 28;
Lisbeth Hjort 12;
Maximilian Stock Ltd. 15.

**Octopus
Publishing Group**
David Munns 105; Emma
Neish 65, 121; Lis Parsons
45, 71, 81, 85, 89, 91, 123;
William Shaw 41, 51, 101,
107, 115; Ian Wallace 67.

Thinkstock
iStockphoto 5, 6, 9, 27.